D0617152

GOLDEN BOY

GOLDEN BOY

the book of a musical by
Clifford Odets & William Gibson
based upon Mr. Odets' play
with lyrics by Lee Adams
to music by Charles Strouse

ATHENEUM   NEW YORK

Published simultaneously in Canada by
McClelland & Stewart Ltd.
Manufactured in the United States of America by
H. Wolff, New York

Designed by Harry Ford

"Division is not our destiny."

THE musical version of GOLDEN BOY was presented by HILLARD ELKINS at the Majestic Theatre, New York City, October 20, 1964, with the following cast of principals:

JOE	*Sammy Davis*
LORNA MOON	*Paula Wayne*
TOM MOODY	*Kenneth Tobey*
ROXY GOTTLIEB	*Ted Beniades*
TOKIO	*Charles Welch*
RONNIE	*Johnny Brown*
WELLINGTON	*Roy Glenn*
ANNA	*Jeannette DuBois*
FRANK	*Louis Gossett*
EDDIE SATIN	*Billy Daniels*
LOPEZ	*Jaime Rogers*

The company of other actors and dancers comprised *Don Crabtree, Bob Daley, Marguerite Delain, Lola Falana, Maxwell Glanville, Buck Heller, Baayork Lee, Theresa Merritt, Terrin Miles, Robbin Miller, Sally Neal, Benny Payne, Harold Pierson, Albert Popwell, Louise Quick, Mabel Robinson, Amy Rouselle, Kenneth Scott, Stephan Taylor, Ralph Vucci, Lamont Washington, and Lester Wilson.*

Sets and costumes by TONY WALTON
Lighting by THARON MUSSER
Musical Director, ELLIOT LAWRENCE
Orchestrations by RALPH BURNS
Choreography by DONALD MCKAYLE
Score published by E. H. MORRIS

The production was directed by ARTHUR PENN.

CONTENTS

GOLDEN BOY

PREFACE: A MEMENTO

SOME ACCOUNT of how and why the unlikely collaboration which follows came into being is perhaps in order.

I first met Clifford Odets in the fall of 1950 when he admitted me to a playwrights' seminar he was organizing at the Actors Studio. I knew much of his work by heart, because in the late thirties Odets was the playwright most of my generation wanted to be, but my knowledge of his plays had not prepared me for the man I met face to face. I lack room here to describe the nature of that fabulous beast—it is a subject for five books, and my wife is writing one of them—but I was dazzled, smitten, and rapt. He was a marvellous and infinitely patient teacher, and I learned more from him than I believed was possible from any man. All winter the seminar met twice a week for sessions of four hours each, and Odets talked most of the time; I had never in my life heard such talk, and never will hear its like again. The potency of spirit in that body was larger than life-size, it was archangel-size, and it was compounded with an element of earth which was tragic, for by that time Clifford was an archangel who had fallen. For reasons he never knew, and despite his offering no word to suggest I had a grain of talent, I felt I owed half my survival that year to Clifford.

After the seminar we kept in touch, politely but impersonally, until in 1953 I found myself employed directing a theatre group of psychiatric patients in the institution where my wife was a member of the psychoanalytic staff; one of the plays we produced for public showing was *Rocket to the Moon*. I knew it was a good play, but we were producing nothing but good plays by the most eminent living playwrights, and *Rocket* was the only text we lived with—our rehearsal schedule consisted of two or three evenings a week, and each production went on for months—over which I was not ready to die of boredom after a few weeks; I could say to our cast in all truth that I thought it as good a play as the country had given birth to, an opinion I have not changed. Clifford came up to see it, courteously told me and the cast he was "very impressed," which he was not, and spent the week-end with us. Upon his return to the city he adopted the habit of phoning us twice a week around eleven at night, to chat for an hour or two about nothing and everything; and thus began a friendship which lasted until his death.

We were among those he asked to see when eleven years later he lay dying in a Hollywood hospital, and because we were on Cape Cod with an unlisted phone the message reached us a week late; I flew out that night. Clifford never knew I was there, he was heavily sedated the last three days and oblivious to this world, but all that week I lived in the rented Beverly Hills house he had occupied, and indeed continued to fill. Its every room was brimful of his voracious spirit, hundreds of masterwork records drowning the piano top and spilling into chairs, a thousand books overflowing the shelves onto tabletops and floors, and everywhere scraps of notepaper overrun by his handscript, jottings to himself in red ink about fictional characters, the conduct of life, women, art and artists, childhood and fatherhood, his own nature, and unsent letters, usually irate. Paula Strasberg was there acting as housekeeper that month, being mother to Clifford's two teen-agers, and I loved her for it, and since it seemed part of my purpose was to familiarize myself with the legacy of problems every death leaves the survivors, I read all I could of what Clifford had last been working on; Paula brought me whatever she could find. In the garden—beside the alluring and baptismal font of moviedom, the swimming pool, used by no one in the household except a girl friend of Clifford's secretary—I read the mimeographed draft of the *Golden Boy* musical with which Clifford had planned to return to the stage.

It was obvious that, at the least, much work remained to be done. The driving line of the original play was of course there; Clifford had once said to me that he "never thought much of that play" but after viewing some semi-pro staging of it years later he "knew they'll never break it down," and his sense of its line was still unerring. But music in the theatre creates a profoundly altered time-world in the audience, material which in straight drama requires ten minutes of preparation can in a musical context be attacked instantly, and the text was that of straight drama, as yet undistilled to the concentrate which music compels. And Clifford, still working on the page, had not been privileged to witness the physical fact onstage of a Negro boy talking to a white girl; Joe Bonaparte had been changed in name only, and to Wellington at that. I rather disapproved of the whole project, which seemed a cashing-in upon the current scene, and it would be a year before I understood what Clifford's eye had seen in it. Nor did I understand the implications I have stated here, I knew only that if this text went into production a swarm of problems would arise and no writer's hand would be there to meet them, it lay dying on a hospital sheet. I had a brief fantasy at that swimming pool of offering my services to the producer Hillard Elkins, whom I did not know, but concluded that my expectation of being indispensable to him would not necessarily coincide with his; I thought if he wanted me he would call me, and a year later he did.

Two days after Clifford's body was cremated I flew back to Massachusetts and my own work. I could not shake his death, and a month later I sat for eight unhappy days over a tape recorder dictating every detail of it I had observed during my week in his house, as well as all I could remember of him in the years preceding, and put the tapes away for whatever interest the future might take in him as man and writer. In the next year we were much involved with his spiritual estate; my wife began the research for her biographical study, and we lived immersed in his papers and other people's memories of him. Some of his physical possessions were always in view around our house, his son had presented me with a few of his pipes and my wife with his silver cigarette case, and we had inherited a quantity of his unwanted books and 78-rpm records, and all winter on our enclosed porch there stood a certain old writing table. It was part of the shambles found in the New York apartment Clifford had lived in with his wife and children prior to her death at the age of thirty-three, and which he had continued to pay the rent on throughout his last nine years in Beverly Hills. The table was too shabby to be sold or given away, and it was to be junked; but when Paula told us it was dear to Clifford because on it he had written his first play, *Awake and Sing!*, my wife harassed me into roping it onto our station-wagon, and we drove it home to Stockbridge. That winter a builder was putting up a workroom for me in the woods by our cottage on Cape Cod, and in mid-summer when I drove my family there the table was back on top of the station-wagon; it went into the new studio as my worktable.

We were hardly there when my wife answered the phone and said, "You want to talk to Hillard Elkins?" I knew *Golden Boy* was in Boston and what the conversation would be, and the next night my wife and I drove in from the Cape to see another show in trouble on the road. I was prepared to say two clever things to whatever writer was with it, and then drive off again, my duty discharged. I was not prepared to find the book gutted of content, no writer present at all, the audience yawning, the director in the third week of a holiday at home in merrie England, and, with its Broadway unveiling a month and a half off, the star in an impotent wrath that the production was saying nothing of what he knew it must say—if only for verisimilitude—on the most divisive issue of our time in this country. I told Elkins that from beginning to end the book, wherever it had a choice of materials, had made the wrong choice; Hilly said it had been a scissors-and-paste job put together by a committee of non-writers after Clifford's death. I was not astounded when that night he and Sammy Davis asked would I rewrite it, but I was deeply unready to say yes.

I had ten motives converging on me to push me in,

all impure, but I made a virtuous effort to surmount
them. I heard that another playwright whom I respected
had been up to see the show, and when Hilly quoted his
opinion, "It ain't nigger enough," I said I quite agreed
and requested Hilly to phone him that moment to invite him to rewrite it, if he accepted I'd be off the hook;
and I went into another room and read a newspaper
until Hilly came in and said I wasn't, the other guy was
in the middle of a play. I said I was in the middle not
only of a play but of a book I had been working on for
three years. I was much attracted to Hilly, a hybrid
original of 34 with a fast wit and insinuating intelli-
gence, part rocket, part goniff, part magus at the cradle
of talent, who understood what Clifford meant to me,
and I could not but admire a host with the chuzpah to
invite a fly and say bring your own flypaper; from our
first handshake we met each other on the level. And
when I listened to Sammy's passionate tongue, which
talked Clifford's language, I saw I was in the presence of
another fast wit and incisive mind, and an ego whose
thousand-horsepower drive was in this hour of history
married to the collective ego of twenty million Ameri-
cans in their assault on the old order for an honorable
place within it. I also met "the boys," the songwriters
Charles Strouse and Lee Adams, who turned out to be
another humorous pair; whatever the show might be
lacking it was not extracurricular jokes, and I knew that
to work with the company would be a pleasure. I could
play savior, learn as a theatre man something of the
nature of musical shows, impersonate my dead mentor—
an act which contained some irrational overtones of
resurrection—and by an assist towards the box-office success of the show repay to his progeny some of my debt to

him. Further, I could speak a few words on a social issue
that moved me more to vehemence than anything had
in two decades. When Sammy said he had "fused Clifford a bit" I quite believed it, because he fused me too,
and now I understood not only Clifford's promise to him
—"I'm going to write this play in your mouth!"—but his
non-fiscal interest in the undertaking: Clifford's theme
had always been the liberation of the soul from its social
shackles, and the Negro now was the equivalent of his
cab-driver of the thirties. One of my deeper doubts was
my capacity to write for and about Negroes, and when
Hilly reminded me that we had "an expert consultant"
in Sammy I said yes, the only way I could envision any
white man daring to take pencil to this would be in collaboration with Sammy on every line; doing so would be
to educate oneself on a sizeable segment of American
life. Sammy's pitch was less abstract, he said pleasantly
that if the show came in as the bookless dud it was he
hoped I would blame myself, and to my wife his parting
word was, "Help!"

Yet my strongest desire to decline came when next
morning I read for the tenth time Clifford's play. My
musical taste is not identical with that of the populace,
and I have never taken an interest in the musicalization
of plays on which our theatre compliments itself as hav-
ing created a new form; its accomplishment seems to me
to consist mainly of replacing good writing with plati-
tudinous music and dance. Half a million dollars was
impotent to do anything more than denature the artwork
Clifford's play had been written as, and rereading it
brought the tears to my eyes, partly because it was his
own obituary, partly because the fire of that writing
could still singe any perceptive reader. People in the

show were saying his dialogue was "dated," simply un-
true, it remained what it always was, the best dialogue
ever written by an American; what they meant was that
dialogue written for a white couple in 1937 was unbe-
lievable in the mouths of a Negro youth and a white
girl in 1964. Measured against what was onstage the play
was such a towering act of genius that I decided there
and then that I would say no, and that conscience—
Clifford's or mine, it wasn't clear—was ordering me back
to my own muse. Yet we stayed over to see the matinee,
and during it I was working out in my head how to re-
store Clifford's story line to the stage, in the knowledge
that if I didn't nobody would. My wife said nothing,
and out of that silence I asked her, "Why do you want
me to do this?" and she said, "I've been asking myself
that question"; our thoughts were not dissimilar.

When we left for the Cape I told Hilly my final
answer was I definitely didn't know, and he must pro-
ceed as though I'd said no; to redo the entire book in the
time available seemed impossible. Still, I took a mimeographed script with me back to my studio. Hilly phoned
the next evening and I said I was sitting with it, call
again tomorrow, and the following day I told him it
could be done and I was doing it, but by then I had rewritten a third of the first act for myself; what finally
ensnared me was the joy of solving and wording. En-
deavoring to write in Clifford's idiom for the sake of a
consistent texture, I worked around the clock, keeping
what was alive onstage, drawing much upon the original
text, and inventing a new body of material for the love
story out of a discovery about the play. Though the
protagonist's dilemma—art or worldly success—was pos-
tulated as a social allegory, its turning point was indi-

vidual, if the woman had not betrayed the boy the
denouement would have evaporated, and this fact was
fraught with meaning for a production whose new element was interracial love; for a Negro, to make good in
the world implied the white world, and if the betrayal
was of love, the allegory had willy-nilly changed into one
of interpenetration of the races. As my wife said, the
Southerners saw the issue with clarity as a sexual matter,
and my own view was that with the act of love ac-
ceptable the racial problem qua racial problem would
vanish; if sex was taboo, so was sitting together at a
lunch counter. Seeing the lovers thus as representatives
of a larger story—I had no question it was how Clifford
would have seen them—I rewrote the first act in five
days and took my illegible pages back into Boston, to
advise Hilly and Sammy that if they wished to go in
this direction I would rewrite the second act and nothing
was lost if they didn't.

My reading of the pages was greeted by a collective
sigh of relief—Sammy said he saw only one problem,
"How you gonna teach Sidney Poitier to sing?" and Lee
Adams said, "Come on, Sammy, he sings pretty good!"
—and only the willingness of the director to collaborate
was in question. When he flew in from London the next
day I found he was not dissatisfied with his present
script and he found he "basically disagreed" with mine;
given a year I might have argued this through, but we had
six weeks, and the next night at my request my almost
brother Arthur Penn was in Boston to inspect the production. It oppressed him—walking from the theatre to
the hotel he shook his head over the labor of "lifting"
it—but he listened attentively to my third reading of my
pages, and when Hilly asked him would he direct Arthur

said simply, "Yes." I bestowed a kiss upon his right
hand, and Sammy and I embraced so collisively that half
of Sammy's drink baptized us both; from that instant,
though I was to suffer moments of perplexity, I never
doubted we would have a show. It was well after mid-
night, and a year to the day when, with his son at his
bedside, I had touched Clifford's hand in farewell and
felt its chill, an hour before his death.

The next afternoon I drove again to the Cape to rewrite the second act; in three days I was done, and when
the following noon I rejoined the show it was to live
with it until we brought it in. Hilly was now undertaking
little less than a complete second production while per-
forming the first, and the events of the subsequent weeks
constituted a breakneck saga—Arthur threw the new
book in its entirety onstage with a week's rehearsal, and
most of the scenery was changed to fit, and Hilly hired
an additional choreographer named Herb Ross who was
invaluable in contributing half-a-showful of new dance
to new songs composed by the boys, and I rewrote the
book for the last time a week before opening night—all
of which was so exhilarating that throughout I paid
Hilly a dollar a day for the privilege of attendance. Day
after day, pages that were in my typewriter at noon were
on the stage that evening, it was a heroic and joyful
company to work with, and it repaid us trebly for
Arthur's initial decision to sustain its morale by firing
nobody. It was never possible for us to bring in a truly
organic show—the components we had to blend, music,
book, casting, lyrics, dance, sets, were so disparate the
union was not unlike a shotgun wedding, and the daily
revisions to meet musical changes cost us much of Clifford's dialogue—and the reviews we garnered reflected

its inner incompatibilities; but however misbegotten it
was alive, and its successful delivery after such labors
displeased none of us. Clifford's son was with us on
opening night, and although after seeing it in Boston he
had planned to picket it with a maledictory banner we
rewrote his opinion too, which meant something to me.

People said that Clifford aloft must be smiling down
upon us; I don't think so, I think the cloud around his
feet is littered with unsent letters in red ink, all irate,
most of them pointing out my inadequacies and the rest
denouncing a higher authority for the omission of mail
service earthwards. I must add that, in a way it em-
barrasses me to recall, I never felt Clifford's ghost was
far off. It hardly escaped me that my baptismal chore
at the table on which he had written his first play was
the unfinished libretto of his last, and on the road my
nightly relaxation was over some of his old records, three
dozen of the more obscure Haydn and Mozart sym-
phonies from the seventies with the dates noted in his
handscript, and any pipe I had in my mouth was one of
the best I owned, those his son had given me. When one
burned through I thought it a bad omen, and saw I had
turned quite superstitious. In our second meeting Hilly
said that Clifford like Moses "had been given the Tablets but not allowed into the promised land," and when
the next day my wife received in the mail an Israeli
solicitation for funds containing a tin miniature of the
Tablets I appropriated it, and wore it pinned inside my
shirt to every rehearsal and performance thereafter; the
one afternoon I forgot it I felt stricken, though no evil
ensued, and I gave it to Sammy an hour before our
Broadway opening, saying I hoped it would work for
him, and of course it did. Such hallucinations ended

with the labors they subserved. Wishes persist longer, and the night the rewritten book first went onstage I received from Hilly the only telegram I was moved to keep; it read, "Thanks from those of us who are here and I'm sure those of us who aren't."

The truth is that my friendship with Clifford was the oddest of my life, in which I believed the respect and love went in one direction, his. Clifford was at once the most human and inhuman man I ever met; I knew that his regard for me and my family was less specific than symbolic, that we signified some kind of unravaged life beyond his hopes, and between adoration and resentment I was always tonguetied with him. It was not until our last conversation that I felt he was unbored with my share in it. In the fall of 1962 we drove to New York for a week-end—Clifford was there for conferences with Hilly and the boys—and he seemed startled that people would undertake a trip with no purpose other than to be with him; we sat in the living room of the Strasbergs until three in the morning, roaring over his talk and tales, and he spent that afternoon with us in an apartment downtown until we were to leave; on the sidewalk we said goodbye till the next time, and we all kissed, and as I drove away from him at the curb my wife beside me said, "Did you see? Clifford was crying."

Two weeks later we had an envelope in that emphatic handscript which for years we loved to see arrive on a letter; it contained one of the charming gouaches Clifford was wont to paint on the backs of postcards, and a note to our boys saying he had made it for them—it was of "two brothers"—and asking them to "tell your Ma and Pa I was very happy that you all drove down, for I know that real friendship made you come." It closed with a postscript to us, "I was very moved that you came to see me and cried a little when you left. That strange street was stranger when your car rolled off."

Tears come easy in our profession, and none of us knew then we would not meet again. It was the following July that we had a last note from Clifford, in an envelope full of stamps addressed to our older boy; he said he was off to the hospital for some x-rays, there were gastric troubles and they didn't know what. My wife wrote him that day, and I added a word saying he should keep us posted, that we were well but I lived as always with my fingers crossed. We had the impulse to phone him, but he was not a man to phone easily, wary, not welcoming calls that intruded on his music or girls or thoughts, always suspicious of what the world wanted from him. I sat late that afternoon at my typewriter thinking about him and his note; I was a little soft-headed with my gin-and-tonic before dinner, and I imagined writing Clifford a letter expressing all he meant to me, telling him I wanted to say I love you, I really love you, I don't know what you will do with this declaration except be embarrassed and encumbered by it, but let me once get it said. I did not type out the letter, of course; what with ambivalences and rebuffs, men sidestep these unmanly avowals. And our next news was the week-late phone call saying he had asked us to come, but was now unconscious and dying.

In his house, the night of his cremation, the last guest to leave was the girl who had been his secretary for five years, and I saw her to the door; we had made our good-byes when she turned to say offhand, "You know he thought the world of you," and I smiled, and have lived

for fifteen months now wanting to cry into that con-
sumed ear no, I didn't know, I didn't know it at all. And
I came home to my book about my dead parents, from
which Hilly's call was to summon me. Thinking back
I see that my indecisiveness in saying yes was only a
seeming, a waiting until I felt words would not fail me,
for in the moment when my wife with the phone in her
hand said, "You want to talk to Hillard Elkins?" something in me knew for a certainty I was taking on Clifford's unfinished business. Surely some of my pleasure
in it was in a last companionship with him, of an ideal
sort, minus the thorns of his totality in the flesh; the
dead are easy to love, unable to speak up for themselves,
and it is precisely how we conceive heaven, populated
by loving spirits purged of the realities of earth.

But in this world every street is a little stranger now,
friend.

W. G.

ACT ONE

1.

No overture.

A spotlight picks out a boxer in a gym; as he shadow-boxes, a rhythm, set up by his sniffs, is picked up quietly by percussion in the orchestra. Another spot hits a second fighter, working out on the big bag; his punches are punctuated by grunts in another rhythm, also picked up by percussion. The two boys are moving in a rhythmic counterpoint when in another spot a third boxer enters skipping rope; his rhythm meshes with the others. As the lights come up, a fourth fighter contributes another rhythm working the pulley-weights, and a fifth another at the speed-bag, and a sixth another at shadow-boxing. Each fighter has his own chant, repeated over and over:

> Don't swallow the mouthpiece,
> Don't swallow the mouthpiece. . . .
>
> Semi-final in the Garden,
> Make a hundred'n fifty bucks,
> Semi-final in the Garden,
> Make a hundred'n fifty bucks. . . .

Keep your chin down!
Keep your chin down! . . .

Left and right and duck and in!
Left and right and duck and in! . . .

Move! Keep moving!
Move! Keep moving! . . .

The counterpoint of rhythms and chants mounts.
When a whistle blows, all the boxers come together in
pairs to spar, a dance which builds to a violent climax
of knockdowns, and then subsides; each dancer returns
to his private act, some drift out, and the gym is quiet
again, two or three boxers working out.

A Negro youth, JOE—*a piece of tape over his eye—*
wanders into the gym, studies one boxer at work, lifts
a finger in hello to another, hanging around until oppo-
site him three white men and a blonde enter; they are
TOM MOODY, ROXY GOTTLIEB, TOKIO, *and* LORNA MOON.
JOE *calls over to* TOM, *his voice empty of any connection*
other than that of business:

JOE: Where's my dough?
BOXER [INDIGNANT]: Who told girls to come in here?
LORNA [A DRY WIT]: Modest? Close your eyes.
TOM: She's my girl.
LORNA: Yeah, I don't count.
TOM [TO JOE]: You'll get it tomorrow. Joe, why won't
    you *hit?*
JOE [CURT]: I beat him on points.
TOM [UNSATISFIED]: Yeah, you got fast hands, very fast
    on your feet, okay, but you don't want to hit—

ROXY [A LOUDMOUTH]: They seen him in five fights now and they don't like him! You read what he wrote in his column, that Drake? "Joe Wellington, the thinking man's fighter!"

JOE: I *think*, what's wrong with that?

ROXY: The people who'll pay to watch a thinker you could fit in a phone booth!

TOM: You pull your punches, Joe, you don't throw your hands right and you don't throw them enough.

JOE [COLD]: I won.

TOM: Yeah, but two minutes out of every round you don't *like* fighting.

ROXY: And *three* minutes he don't like hitting!

TOM: This job needs a hundred per cent enthusiasm, all your time and thoughts. What's bothering you?

JOE [IMPASSIVE]: I don't know what you mean, Mr. Moody.

TOM: Looks? Some boys'll lose a fight to keep their nose intact—

JOE: My looks don't interest me.

LORNA [PLEASANTLY]: Liar.

(JOE *shoots her a look as she drifts past him; she interests him.*)

JOE: Who's a liar?

LORNA: Everybody I know.

TOM: Now you're going to meet Grant next week, he's a good boy and—

JOE: Not as good as you think.

TOM [DISPLEASED]: Oh?

JOE: He pulls your lead, hesitates a second, then he's in. Catch that second, he's open for a right.

TOM: And what do you do with his left hook?

JOE: Avoid it.

TOM: Well. You're a pretty clever boy—

ROXY: He's clever, he's fast, but he's first-class lousy in the shipping department!

TOKIO [A PATIENT SOUL]: Roxy, cut it out.

ROXY: I bought a piece of him, I got a right to say it! What is he, scared?

JOE [HEAD IN, ICY]: Mr. Gottlieb, you bought a piece of my contract, not of me.

ROXY [HEAD BACK]: What?

JOE: Point two, don't call me *him*, I have a name. I call you Mr. Gottlieb, you do the same, please.

(*He walks away.*)

ROXY [FLUSTERED]: What's he want me to do, call him Mr. Gottlieb?

(JOE *comes back to* TOM, *and* ROXY *hides behind him.*)

JOE: Point three, I win for you, don't I? Whyn't you be as quick with my dough as you are with the needles?

(*He walks away again, and out.*)

TOM [SHOUTS]: That's how you take criticism? For Christ sake, Roxy!

ROXY [BACKS OFF]: I think I'll slip across the street and pick up lunch.

TOM: Order some brains!

(ROXY *departs in a hurry.*)

TOKIO: Tom, that boy knows his own needs. He has to think he's the best thing ever walked in shoe leather.

TOM: He thinks so now!

TOKIO [GENTLY]: No, he don't. He's a colored boy, Tom, we don't let him. It's front.

(TOM *in dissatisfaction turns, passing the boxer at the big bag with an irritable comment—"Throw your hands!"—and* LORNA *and* TOKIO *follow him off.*)

2.

As the gym moves out the WELLINGTON *kitchen moves in, a workingclass room in Harlem. Present around the table are* WELLINGTON, RONNIE, ANNA *folding clothes, and* FRANK *with a newspaper.*

RONNIE [A CLOWN]: Don't change the subject, ole man. Buy me a cab, I'll pay it off by the week. Joe takes the night shift, I'm a married man so I don't take the night shift—

WELLINGTON [AMUSED]: No cab.

RONNIE: Don't you wanna help your own family? Joe's your son, he can drive like a fire engine—

WELLINGTON: That's why he don't get a cab.

ANNA: Come to bed, Ronnie.

RONNIE: Looka your daughter, slavin' for this bunch of lazy spooks, a fine life for an intelligent chick—

WELLINGTON: She's my daughter but she's your wife, she ain't so intelligent as you say.

RONNIE: How much you got in the bank, three grand?

WELLINGTON: Millions.

FRANK [READING]: What's it your business how much he's got? Go to bed.

RONNIE: I wanna take your sister outa the kitchen, where's the gratitude?

(FRANK *pats his bulging belly.*)

I'm warnin' everybody here, if matters go from worse to worse don't expect me to support this family! I'm warnin' you!

ANNA: Come to bed.

WELLINGTON: We have receive the warnin'. Go to bed.

ANNA: Come to bed, Ronnie.

RONNIE: Go to bed, come to bed, what the hell's so special in bed?

(JOE *drifts in, eye still taped.* WELLINGTON's *manner changes in relation to him, more troubled.*)

JOE: Hi. How come you ain't in bed, Ronnie?

WELLINGTON: What's the matter with your eye, Joe?

JOE [EVASIVE]: Had a fight last night—some cat in the park—

WELLINGTON: He hit you?

JOE: No, he kissed me on the brow.

WELLINGTON: Stay outa them street fights, Joe.

JOE [BORED]: Yes, Pa.

WELLINGTON: Oughta find somethin' better to do than hang around them corners.

JOE [BORED]: Yes, Pa.

WELLINGTON: Never knew anybody walk off so many jobs. Why'd you quit the factory, you coulda gone up—

JOE: Goddamit, Pa, you want me to live like a dead man?

WELLINGTON: Want you to live respectable, not be a bum. Whatta y'expect outa life—

JOE: Me! Brother!

(*He takes half the newspaper from* FRANK, *in disgust.*)

What's *new* in the world?

FRANK: Very hot in Alabama, read it and weep. See you in the morning before I leave, Pop.

WELLINGTON: Goin' down there again?

FRANK: Birmingham. They got trouble—

(*He freezes over his half of the newspaper.*)

WELLINGTON: Ain't your trouble—

RONNIE: I got trouble in Harlem. One cab!

FRANK: Pop, you better brace yourself.

WELLINGTON: What?

FRANK: Joe's had a prizefight.

(JOE *comes for the newspaper,* FRANK *holds it off.*)

"Joe Wellington won on points in six—"

WELLINGTON [SMILES]: Must be some other boy, eh, Joe?

(*All wait on* JOE, *who cannot escape, and brazens it out.*)

JOE: Well, what are you gonna do about it?

WELLINGTON [PUZZLED]: Joe, it's you?

JOE: It's me.

FRANK: When'd you turn gladiator?

JOE [SUDDEN VEHEMENCE]: Mind your business! I see you once a year, freedom fighter, what do you know about me?

WELLINGTON [CALMING]: Hey, wait a minute—

JOE: I don't wanna be criticized! In twenty minutes I made a hundred and fifty bucks!

FRANK: What?

RONNIE: You honest to God had a fight?

JOE: Five.

ANNA: Five!

FRANK: Where'd you pick up fighting?

JOE: Downstairs, x-ray eyes. Uptown, downtown, all over this red-white-and-blue-get-your-black-ass-outa-here town—

WELLINGTON: Joe, boy, you *wanna* fight?

JOE [SUDDENLY QUIET]: I don't know. When I fight nobody spits on me, in that ring I'm as good as I am, no previous condition of servitude—

WELLINGTON [TROUBLED]: But be a fighter, Joe, that ain't your nature. Why you wanna fight?

JOE: You know my nature?

WELLINGTON: You know your Ma wanted you to amount to somethin', not be just another colored fighter—

JOE [FLARING]: Poppa, I'm alive! Let me decide once what *I* want to decide!

(JOE *swings away, and the lights dim on the kitchen disappearing, with* WELLINGTON *asking his question a last time:*)

WELLINGTON: Why you wanna fight—

3.

The rooftop of the tenement forms around JOE, and he sings "Night Song":

JOE:
>   Summer,
>   Not a bit of breeze,
>   Neon signs are shining
>   Through the tired trees,
>   Lovers
>   Walking to and fro,
>   Everyone has someone
>   And a place to go.
>
>   Listen,
>   Hear the cars go past,
>   They don't even see me,
>   Flying by so fast,
>   Moving,
>   Going who knows where,
>   Only thing I know is
>   I'm not going there.
>
>   Where do you go
>   When you feel that your brain is on fire?

Where do you go
When you don't even know
What it is you desire?
Listen!
Laughter everywhere.
Hear it!
Life is in the air. . . .

As the night comes
And the town awakes,
Sound of children calling
And the squeal of brakes,
Music,
But a lonely song
When you can't help wond'ring
Where do I belong?

Where do you turn
When you burn with this feeling of rage?
Who do you fight
When you want to break out
But your skin is your cage?
Uptown—
Just another joe,
Downtown—
Where you gonna go? . . .

Always looking
For a place to be,
Where's the bright tomorrow
For a guy like me?

God damn!
Life is going by!
And I stand and wonder
Who the hell am I?

4.

The rooftop gives place to TOM MOODY's office, where
TOM is greeted by a shoeshine boy entering:

BOY: Shine, Mr. Moody?

(TOM gives his foot to the boy's box; the boy
works.)

How's the boxin' business?
TOM [SCATHINGLY]: Wonderful.

> Everything's great,
> Couldn't be better,
> Up to my ears in debt!
> Rent's overdue,
> Nothing but worries—
> How great can things get?
>
> Here I am,
> Thomas J. Moody,
> Three-year-old suit
> From Robert J. Hall,
> Jesus H. Christ!

> *Where am I heading?*
> *These lucky feet*
> *Find the one street*
> *That's guaranteed*
> *To lead to a brick wall!*

(*He gives the listening boy a coin; the boy gives him one back.*)

BOY [COMPASSIONATE]: Keep the change. Jeez!

(*He exits, and* TOM *smacks his brow.*)

TOM:

> *Ev'ry old horse*
> *Has to win sometime,*
> *When is it my big purse?*
> *Things have to change,*
> *Gotta get better,*
> *They could not get worse!*

(LORNA *enters, dangling her purse; her manner is world-weary and bored.*)

Thought you were home packing your clothes.

LORNA: You want that, baby? I'll disappear like the Indians.

TOM: No, *you* said you had a good mind to leave me—

LORNA: I said I'm damn tired of it and I don't like it, I want to get married—

TOM: Go home, Lorna, gimme some air! It's enough I got my wife on my neck!

(*The phone rings.*)

If that's for me tear it up, I'm not in to God.

LORNA [PICKS IT UP]: Hello?

(*She extends it to* TOM.)

It's Mrs. God.

TOM [INTO PHONE]: Yeah, Monica. . . . Yeah, Monica. . . .

(LORNA *sings to* TOM *and the phone; he twists to hold it out of earshot.*)

LORNA:

> *Here I am,*
> *Still getting nowhere,*
> *Making believe*
> *It's all so divine—*

TOM: *How* much money?

LORNA:

> *Had to get hung*
> *On Mister Married.*
> *Doing things right,*
> *That's not my line,*
> *Screwing things up,*
> *That's where I shine!*

TOM [HANGS UP]: Goodbye! Damn!

> *Just what I need,*
> *She's gonna kill me!*
> *Milking me dry, my wife!*

BOTH:

> *Everything's great,*
> *Couldn't be better!*

TOM:

> *Birds are singing—*

LORNA:

      Vultures, baby—

TOM:

      Flowers blooming—

LORNA:

      Poison ivy—

BOTH:

      What a perfect life!

TOM: She wants five thousand dollars to give me the divorce.

    (LORNA *smiles.*)

What's so funny?

LORNA: Baby, I can let you have a ten.

TOM [STUNG]: When I get rid of Monica we'll get married, do I have to give you a bang on the nose to make you understand?

LORNA: Go to hell.

    (TOM *is choked up;* LORNA *sees and softens.*)

But come back tonight.

TOM [COMES TO HER HAND]: Honey, don't leave me, don't ever leave me. If I had the cash I'd—buy you the White House!

LORNA [WEARILY]: Who'd cut the grass?

    (JOE *and* TOKIO *appear in the doorway, unseen by* TOM.)

TOM: If ole black Joe beats Grant next week I'll take you to the Plaza.

(He follows LORNA's *gaze to* JOE, *who stands eyeing him;* TOM *is embarrassed.)*

Oh. Hiya—come on in—

JOE [NOT MOVING]: Where's my dough?

TOM [FISHES IN HIS POCKET]: Yeah, well, I picked up your purse, there's not much left, Joe. You owe me a hundred and thirty.

(He gives a bill to JOE, *who stares at it in his hand.)*

JOE: Whaat?

TOM: Gym fees, mouthpiece, taping, two advances—I bought that columnist a dinner to mention your win—

(He hands JOE *a paper;* JOE *scans it.)*

It's all itemized.

JOE: How come I never win with you?

TOM: What kind of a crack is that?

JOE: What kind of money is this? Twenty bucks out of a hundred fifty, I'd do better to scrub your floor!

TOKIO [STUDIES IT]: It's a true bill, Joe.

JOE: Twelve bucks for dinner, what'd he eat, the whole cow?

(He jerks his head at LORNA.)*

Was she there?

TOM: What the hell business—

JOE: I just like to know who's eating on me!

TOM [ANGRY]: Here's a ten, I'll pay for your publicity!

(*He throws a bill at* JOE, *and it falls to the floor;
nobody moves,* TOM *and* JOE *staring at each other.*)

Pick it up.

JOE: Anybody calls me ole black Joe I don't stoop for,
Mr. Moody.

(LORNA *rises, stoops, smooths out the bill, and
proffers it to* JOE.)

LORNA: I *was* there.

JOE [NOT TAKING IT, A PAUSE]: Give it back to him, Miss
Moon. Next time I buy you a meal I'd like the
pleasure of your company.

(*He turns to go, then back to* TOM.)

Don't count on me meeting Grant next week,
maybe I'll give up fighting as a bad job.

(*He walks out.*)

LORNA [IMPRESSED]: Hey, hey.

TOKIO: Got a lot of pride, Tom.

TOM [DISGUSTED]: So's the Queen of England, who'd
she ever beat?

TOKIO: I'd like to take him on a road tour, get some
real wins under his belt. Joe can make as good a
lightweight as I've trained—

TOM: Not if he won't fight!

LORNA [PAUSE]: You want that boy to fight?

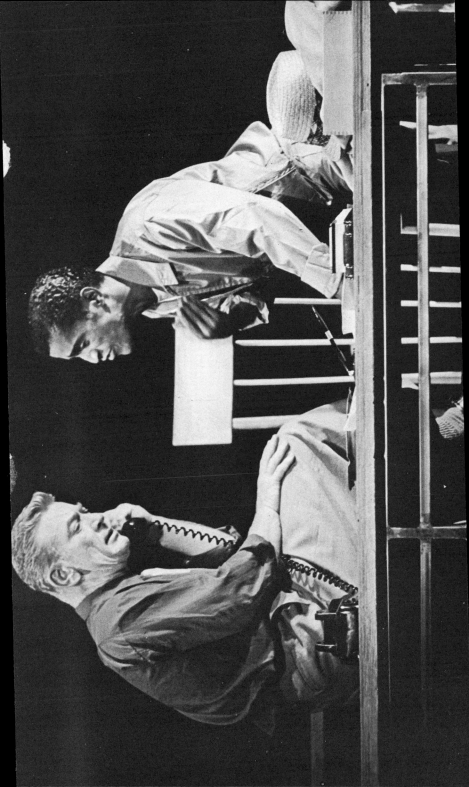

TOM: Do I want to see tomorrow? Do you want to get married, Miss Moon? For the dough that's in a winner I'd make Niagara Falls go back to Canada!

LORNA: Okay.

(*She takes up her purse.*)

I'll make him fight.

TOM: How?

LORNA: I'll think of something, baby, book the tour.

(*She wanders out, singing in a spot as the office vanishes:*)

> *Leave it to me,*
> *Little Miss Fixit,*
> *Things'll work out just fine.*
> *I spend my life*
> *Solving his problems.*
> *When will I solve mine?*

5.

A schoolyard playground moves in; a Negro boy is on a bench with a cigarette. JOE walking through eyes him with disapproval.

BOY:

> Beer and whiskey,
> Whiskey and beer,
> Makes your head start achin',
> Makes your eyes unclear.
> Makes you waste your money,
> Turns you blind and dumb—

JOE [TAKES CIGARETTE]:

> Gimme some.

BOY:

> Strong tobacco,
> Cigarette smoke,
> Such a dirty habit
> Makes you damn near choke—

JOE:

> Fills your lungs with poison,
> Makes your brain go numb—

BOY [SNATCHES CIGARETTE BACK]:

> Gimme some!

JOE:

>   *Will you ever get smart?*

BOY:

>   *I doubt it.*
>   *Tell me somethin's bad and I can't live*
>   *Without it—*

(*He runs out with the cigarette.* LORNA *has saun-tered in.*)

LORNA [DRAWLS]: Evening, Mr. Gottlieb.

JOE [TURNS]: Well, now. Miss—Moon over Harlem. What are you doing uptown with the animals?

LORNA: Animals?

(JOE *thumbs at the tenements around.*)

Oh. I've got a lot of problems, honey, none of which is black and white. I was looking for you.

JOE [CLIPPED]: Why?

LORNA: Offer me a chair, Mr. Wellington.

JOE [CLIPPED]: Why look for me?

LORNA: Well—

(*She looks* JOE *in the eye, smiles.*)

I told Moody I'd make you fight.

JOE: How will you do that, Miss Moon?

LORNA: To tell you the truth, I—

(*She appraises him, decides how.*)

—think I'll tell you the truth.

JOE [SMILES]: Have a chair, lady.

(*He indicates the bench;* LORNA *sits, and he wanders.*)

You always tell the truth?

LORNA [CALMLY]: No, I lie when it works. The boys want to take you on a road tour.

JOE: Nice of them.

LORNA: Interested?

JOE: Not much. Maybe I'll be a big TV star, a road tour might spoil my looks.

LORNA: You think you're ugly.

(JOE *halts, to contemplate her.*)

JOE: You don't?

LORNA: Truth or consequences, I did till I heard you talk, you got prettier every minute.

JOE [DRY]: Same to you, tell me more.

LORNA: Moody thinks you can be a winner.

JOE: Yeah. It's more than I think of Moody, he's a born loser if I ever saw one. That's what interests you in him, huh?

LORNA [BLINKS, CHANGES TACK]: Well. Go on a tour, see the country— Ever travel?

JOE: Sure, thousands of miles, all in Harlem.

(*He comes to her on the bench.*)

Look, your Mr. Moody sees me like *this*—

(*Fists clenched, as if to fight.*)

—but inside I'm three other guys, I only learned this to get through the streets. In the ring my hands don't *leave* me. Hit and you get hit, you're open for it, is that a happy life? Anyway, if I make Mr. Moody rich he won't be your type, so do him a favor, tell him I said no. It's just not my instinct to fight.

LORNA [PAUSE]: You always tell the *half*-truth?

(JOE *is stopped by this, moves away, and stares out front over the audience.*)

JOE [THEN]: Okay, the other half. My poppa's a junk-man and thinks that's fine, my brother works for CORE and gets his head kicked in—and *my* whole life seems like one long night I've been standing in alleys looking across the park at these buildings, the lights of this city, my God, it's like diamonds in the air, why can't *I* pick some too? Who lives there, angels? white angels in robes? I'll tell you a half-truth—

(*He is interrupted by two Negro boys fleeing through the playground; three white* PUNKS *stalk in after them.*)

PUNKS: Get outa this playground! Beat it, boogies! Whatta y'think, we pay taxes to give you little bastards a free ride? Get offa the swing! Frig off, ya friggin' monkeys!

(*One* PUNK *comes down to* LORNA *and* JOE.)

Whatta, y'like coons, lady?

(JOE *takes* LORNA's *arm to leave, but the* PUNKS *are around him.*)

JOE: Look, fellas, let's cool it, huh?

(*He starts out with* LORNA.)

PUNK: Hands offa the lady, nigger!

(*The* PUNK *swings at* JOE, *who ducks and counterpunches, and the* PUNK *is on his butt; the other two rush* JOE, JOE *staggers one but the second climbs his back, pinning him while another socks him; now three Negro* PUNKS *spill into the playground from the opposite side and join in the brawl, which becomes general, even* LORNA *hitting one* PUNK *on the head with her purse, until the Negroes and boys chase after the three whites out of the playground; this burst of brawl is fast, on and off in half a minute, then quiet again.* JOE *stumbles back from the pursuit to find* LORNA *on her knees; she and* JOE *have had the breath knocked out of them.*)

JOE [WITH SOME HUMOR]: My poppa—tells me stay out of street-fights. You okay?
LORNA: Oh, sure—happens every day—

(*She picks up articles from her purse, and* JOE *comes to help her.*)

JOE: It does!
LORNA: I'll tell you a secret, your hands left you.

JOE: Yeah. For no reason.

(*Their hands after the same article touch;* JOE *pulls back, and* LORNA's *eye is quizzical.*)

LORNA: Three at one blow and girls scare you?
JOE [LOW]: White girls.

(LORNA *snaps her purse, rises, studies him.*)

LORNA: In the ring the reason is called fame and fortune.
JOE: Yeah. Or twenty bucks from Moody and end up punchy, shining shoes, like Beau Jack.
LORNA: Or live like your poppa, be a junkman in this Garden of Eden.

(*She stares out front over the audience.*)

Angels don't live there, just the rich and famous, and it's better than heaven, you can *fight* your way in.

(*She turns back to him.*)

I like a man whose hands leave him, why don't you reach up and pick a diamond?

(*Their eyes meet: now they are talking about each other.*)

Fight your way in or stay down here on your knees, scaredycat.
JOE [RISES]: And when I'm up there, Miss Moon, where will—you, for instance, be sparkling?

LORNA: I'll be there.

JOE: With Mr. Moody.

(Pointedly:)

You go along with him on road tours?

LORNA [FLAT]: I go along with him.

JOE: You love him?

LORNA [PAUSE]: He's got funny taste, he loves me.

JOE: You love the man?

LORNA: I take good care of little boys, Joe, I never met a man.

JOE (PAUSE): Okay, tell him something for me. I make up my own mind to fight, don't send more ladies. And I won't slug and be slugged, but if he wants the best *boxer* in the business I'll—

(He hesitates.)

LORNA: Yes?

JOE [DECIDES]: I'll give him three minutes of fighting per round on a road tour.

LORNA [PAUSE]: I'll be all eyes.

JOE: I'll dazzle them for you.

> *Stick around,*
> *Things are gonna happen.*
> *Fireworks—*
> *Stick around and see!*
>
> *Watch me in the arena,*
> *Eat crackerjack*
> *While I'm smack-*

ing some hack
For a fee!

Stick around!
You can hold the basket,
While I shake
That money tree!

And of course
In certain cases
A dark horse
May win some races.
Stick around, lady, and see!

Tell Moody that when you're—in his arms tonight.
LORNA: You're a fresh kid.
JOE: You're just used to stale ones.

Stick around
And you'll see some action.
Who can tell
What the kid'll do?

Here I go after diamonds,
And I'll come back
With a sack-
full and toss
You a few!

Stick around!
You can shine my trophies,
Lead the cheers
When they shout for me.

There won't be nobody hotter,
I want the whole enchilada,
And if I come up a winner,
Brotherhood Week—take me to dinner!
Stick around, lady, and—

See the boy
Who's gonna fight now!
See the boy
Start movin' right now!
Stick around, lady, and see!

I'll take you to a cab.

(*They leave the playground together.*)

6.

The playground changes to a Harlem street scene. RONNIE and some cronies and girls are hanging around, and FRANK and JOE appear among them. EDDIE SATIN, an elegantly dressed Negro, strolls in and is met by a man who slips him a paper bag; EDDIE takes money out of it.

EDDIE: Next time use a clean envelope.

(A woman crosses with a baby carriage.)

How's the baby?

(The woman reaches in the carriage, and slips EDDIE money out of it. Another man crosses to give EDDIE money and as EDDIE starts away one bill floats to the street; RONNIE scoops it up.)

RONNIE: Mr. Satin! Mr. Satin!
EDDIE [OVER HIS SHOULDER]: Keep it, kid.

(He strolls off.)

RONNIE: The Robin Hood of Harlem!
1ST CRONY: The biggest hood of Harlem!

2ND CRONY: Yeah, steals from the poor and lives rich
down town in that penthouse.

FRANK: But he never forgets he's colored. He misses us
all so much he comes back every day, just to keep
in contact with his ethnic group.

RONNIE: My god is success, need I say more? Joe, make
enough dough to buy your brother-in-law a new
cab!

1ST CRONY: You gonna make the old neighborhood
famous, hey, Joe?

JOE: Sure, nobody ever heard of Harlem till now.

RONNIE: When you're downtown sippin' champagne
with your high-class white friends don't forget
this gawgeous environment which moulded your
character. Don't forget your *roots!*

*Don't forget One Hundred and Twenty-seventh
Street—*

CRONIES:

Don't forget your happy Harlem home!
*Don't forget One Hundred and Twenty-seventh
Street—*

RONNIE:

No, siree! There's no slum like your own!

JOE:

I remember winter evenings at the window,
Watching the evictions in the snow—

ALL:

Oh, no, Joe!
*Don't forget One Hundred and Twenty-seventh
Street—*

RONNIE:

A little bit o' heaven—

ALL:

> *Wherever you may go!*

RONNIE:

> *Don't forget the cultural life on this here street—*

ALL:

> *Richer than the outside world suspects!*

2ND CRONY:

> *Hark! the cheerful patter of all the junkies' feet—*

JOE:

> *And the soothing tones of Malcolm X!*

RONNIE:

> *Each night we hasten to our spotless subway,*
> *Riding home is always such a treat—*

> *(They pretend to mug him.)*

> *Don't do that!*

ALL:

> *Don't forget your beautiful old ancestral home—*

RONNIE:

> *An angel named it Harlem—*

ALL:

> *Called One-Two-Seven Street!*

> (RONNIE *does a dance step.*)

JOE: Ronnie, now that I've seen you dance I am firmly convinced we ain't all born with it. Where you spending your winter vacation?

RONNIE: I think I'll go to Florida.

JOE: Why Florida?

RONNIE: Well, when I'm sittin' in my easy chair in front of the television, a friendly man keeps saying, "Hi, there! Come on down!"

ALL:
> *Remember moonlight on the Harlem River—*

JOE:
> *And the cops all strolling two by two—*

ALL:
> *Oh, no, Joe!*
> *Don't forget One Hundred and Twenty-seventh*
>   *Street—*

JOE:
> *Our dandy little ghetto—*

ALL:
> *Whatever you may do!*

GIRLS:
> *Don't forget One Hundred and Twenty-seventh*
>   *Street,*
> *Here where you were born and raised and fed—*

WOMAN:
> *Even as a baby you always smiled so sweet—*

JOE:
> *When the falling plaster hit my head!*
> *Sure, when I'm driving in my big Ferrari,*
> *With some luscious rich chick as my pet,*
> *Believe me,*
> *How I'll miss this beautiful*
>   *Twenty-seventh Street—*
>
> Ladies and gentlemen, I assure you—
>
> *I'll miss it every chance I get!*

TWO BOYS:
> *Don't forget our glorious P.S. Forty-two,*
> *With the ninety kids in every class,*
> *Radiators full of ice all winter through—*

1ST BOY:

> Man, oh, man, you really freeze your a—

(JOE *covers his mouth.*)

RONNIE:

> H is for the heroin they sell here—

JOE:

> A is for the alleys where kids play—

RONNIE:

> R is for the rats that run pell-mell here—

JOE:

> L is for the landlords far away—

RONNIE:

> E is for the endless clean-up projects—

JOE:

> M is for the mouldy roofs above—

JOE & RONNIE:

> Put them all together, they spell Harlem—

RONNIE:

> Oh, yeah—

JOE:

> The place that white folks—
> Think we love!

ALL:

> One-Two-Seven Street!
> One-Two-Seven Street!
> One-Two-Seven Street!

(*The entire streetful begins to dance, takes off on a big circle snaking around, and culminates in a mass twist until* JOE *breaks it.*)

JOE:

> *Cause when I'm far away in some strange city,*
> *All alone and feeling mighty blue—*

ALL:

> *Oh, no, Joe!*
> *Don't forget One Hundred and Twenty-seventh*
>   *Street,*
> *For a Hundred and Twenty-seventh Street will*
>   *never forget—*

JOE:

> *The neighborhood is classy,*
> *We got rats as big as Lassie!*

ALL:

> *Seventh Street will never forget—*

RONNIE: *Keep your mink and ermine,*
>   *We got fifty kinds of vermin!*

ALL:

> *Seventh Street will never forget—*

JOE:

> *We got a right to howl,*
> *We got Adam Clayton Powell!*

ALL:

> *Seventh Street will never forget—*
> *You!*
> *Oh, yeah!*

> *(They shake* JOE's *hand in goodbye, and dance out*
> *as the lights fade.)*

7.

The WELLINGTON *kitchen materializes, with a suitcase in sight on the table. The family is sitting around* LORNA, *embarrassed by this white girl in their home.*

LORNA [LOOKS AT WATCH]: I said I'd—have him there before he changes his mind—

RONNIE: Yeah. I couldn't believe it till I seen him fight, Miss Moon. You never know what somebody's got in him—like the man with the germs, suddenly he's under the knife, haha—

LORNA: Joe's road tour will be good for him—

WELLINGTON: Mebbe so, miss, mebbe so.

(*He walks out.*)

RONNIE [CALLS AFTER HIM]: Ole man, don't spoil the occasion! Joe's fightin' cause he's sick of bein' invisible, this is America, money talks, don't knock it! We're thinkin' of sendin' the ole man to a leper colony.

(*He guffaws, till* ANNA *cuffs the back of his head.*)

ANNA [TERSE]: Don't my husband say funny things, Miss
    Moon? Married seven years and I haven't stopped
    laughin'.

(JOE *comes in, to pack the suitcase.*)

LORNA: I don't think your poppa likes me.

JOE: No, you just—look pale in this light—

ANNA: My father likes everybody, he's a very deep man.

JOE: Yeah, so deep I get lost in him.

ANNA [HELPING AT SUITCASE]: This is the first time Joe
    ever went travellin', he don't know how to pack—

(WELLINGTON *returns, hands* JOE *a sweater.*)

WELLINGTON: You forgot your good sweater.

(*They look at each other, for a wordless moment.*)

JOE [PACKS IT]: Thanks.

LORNA: Question is, do you like me, yes or yes?

WELLINGTON: You all right. Mebbe.

LORNA [MOCK ARCH]: I like your children, now do you
    like me?

WELLINGTON: Yeah. You gonna travel on this train with
    my Joe?

LORNA: I'm a—friend of his manager's—

WELLINGTON: You in favor of Joe prizefightin'?

LORNA: If it gets him what he wants.

WELLINGTON [TROUBLED]: What do he want, be a big
    shot with white folks where he don't belong? I
    wanna see Joe happy, he ain't gonna find it where
    nobody loves him 'less he wins all the time—

(JOE *fingers a new scarf in the suitcase, wrapped in tissue.*)

JOE: What's this?
WELLINGTON: I bought you that, Joe, goin' away present.

(JOE'*s eyes fill.*)

Take it along.
LORNA [INTENT]: We better not miss the train—
WELLINGTON: Use it, keep your neck warm.

(JOE'*s eyes never leave him, with all that is unsaid between them.*)

Have a good trip—eat good—
JOE: Poppa, I got to do this.
WELLINGTON: Take care of yourself—
JOE: Poppa, give me the word—
WELLINGTON: What word?
JOE: Give me the word to go ahead. You're looking at yesterday, I see tomorrow. You want me to spend my whole goddam life in Harlem, like you—with you—
WELLINGTON: Oh, Joe, shut your mouth—
JOE: Give me the word to go ahead!
WELLINGTON: Take care of yourself—
JOE [FIERCELY]: I want you to give me the word!
WELLINGTON [BURSTING OUT]: No! No word! You gonna fight, all right, okay, but I ain't givin' you no word! No!
JOE [LONG PAUSE]: That's how you feel, Poppa?
WELLINGTON: That's how I feel!

(*They stare, each close to tears.* JOE *then slams his suitcase shut, kisses* ANNA, *shakes* RONNIE'S *hand, and on his way out halts passing his father; suddenly he drops the suitcase, and they clutch each other in an embrace.* JOE *takes the suitcase upstage, and the lights dim on the kitchen moving out.*)

8.

___

A suggestion of railroad depot comes in around JOE
with his suitcase, at a distance upstage from LORNA.
When TOM enters with two suitcases, LORNA takes a step
back from him, pointing after JOE.

LORNA: I got him on the train, okay?

TOM: Listen, Monica was pretty friendly last night—

LORNA: Who cares?

TOM: What's the matter with you?

LORNA [THROUGH HER TEETH]: I don't—like—

TOM: She met some bum from Brooklyn, maybe she'll
talk divorce—

LORNA: Tell her don't bother, I'll marry the bum for
you!

TOM [PERPLEXED]: Huh?

LORNA [BITTER]: Anything. Anything for you, baby.

TOM [SIMPLY]: I know that, honey. Every day I tell myself Lorna's here, and—I don't have to thank you,
do I?

LORNA [PAUSE]: No.

(TOM kisses her fingers, and starts off with the suitcases; he looks back as LORNA's song begins, and

with JOE *watching from his distance* LORNA *sings
with a divided mind between the two men, until*
TOKIO *entering takes* JOE *off and* TOM *also leaves.)*

Lorna's here and she's gonna stay.
Lorna's here and baby, she won't go away.

All my talk of leaving
Is only talk,
I'm much too dumb
To take that walk.

Try to lose me, honey, just try.
Lorna's here forever, you big ugly guy!

It's so sad it's funny,
I need you the way you need me . . .
I don't always show it,
But I'm yours, you know it,
Lorna's here where Lorna should be.

Momma's here to hold you,
So like it or not you've got me . . .
Maybe I can't do much,
But when things get too much,
Lorna's here where Lorna should be.

(She walks off to the train.)

9.

The road tour which now begins takes place "in limbo,"
that is, neutral ground on which vignettes are separated
and unified by changes of spotlight.

First we see LORNA, TOM, and ROXY on a train seat.

TRIO:
> Harrisburg Saturday,
> Allentown next week,
> Then a fight in Erie on the first.
> I hate Allentown
> But Erie's the worst!

(Opposite them a crowd of fight fans has gathered,
and turns thumbs down.)

CROWD:
> Boo!

TRIO:
> He won but they don't like him.
> He won but they don't care!
> He's gotta get in there and slug
> To get somewhere!

> *If he would hit!*
> *If he would hit!*
> *If only Joe*
> *Would learn to hit!*

CROWD [AGAIN]:

> *Booooo!*

TRIO:

> *Cleveland Tuesday,*
> *Dayton Friday,*
> *Then a tough ten-rounder in South Bend.*
> *South Bend's bad enough*
> *But Dayton's the end!*

(Fade out on train seat; the crowd disappears. In a spotlight two fighters and JOE *in fight togs dance in, shadow-boxing.)*

1ST FIGHTER: Where you from, baby?

JOE: New York.

2ND FIGHTER: These coal miners are tough, you come a long way to get your face rearranged—

JOE: Hell, any change is an improvement!

(They dance out. Another spot finds a TRAIN CONDUCTOR *passing* ROXY.)

CONDUCTOR: St. Paul, St. Paul, this way out for St. Paul—

ROXY: I got a fat chance of getting a decent pastrami sandwich in a place called St. Paul!

(They walk out. JOE *entering another spot sees* LORNA *at a distance; she does not see him. He sings a fragment of a song, softly:)*

JOE:

>*I wanna be with you,*
>*I wanna be with you—*

(He is interrupted by ROXY *and* TOKIO, *who slap his back and hurry him offstage;* JOE *dances in and out as in a fight,* ROXY *and* TOKIO *crouching to watch. Opposite a spot finds* EDDIE SATIN *on a raised platform, watching the fight intently.)*

ROXY & TOKIO:

>*He's mighty fast,*
>*You must admit,*
>*He could be champ*
>*If he would hit!*
>*I'd have the champ!*
>*I'd make a pile!*
>*He's got the speed!*
>*He's got the style!*

*(*JOE *hurtles in onto his butt, a knockdown, but he is up again on his toes, back into the fight.)*

EDDIE: Takes a good punch, takes a very good punch!

*(*EDDIE *remains visible throughout. The* CONDUCTOR *reappears in another spot with* LORNA.)*

CONDUCTOR: First visit to our fair city, lady?
LORNA: No, I come to Akron every chance I get.

(They walk out separately.)

EDDIE:

> *That's a good boy,*
> *That's a good good boy,*
> *A real sweet boy—*

(*In another spot* JOE *dances in, punching alternately at* TOKIO's *palms;* TOM *and* ROXY *urge him on.*)

TOM: Okay, Joe, you're in the home stretch!
ROXY: You really gotta work hard now!
TOM: Now the big bag!

(*The big bag slides in, and* JOE *turns to punch at it.*)

ROXY: To the stomach! To the stomach! I like a good left to the stomach!

(JOE *without breaking rhythm hits* ROXY *in the stomach, and dances off into another fight.* EDDIE *watching moves with it, his excitement increasing.*)

EDDIE:

> *Hit him! Hurt him!*
> *Yeah, baby!*
> *Pretty, pretty,*
> *Yeah, baby!*
> *Get him! Kill him!*
> *Go, baby!*
> *Go, baby! Oh, baby!*
> *Yeah!*

(*In a spotlight now* JOE, *in slow motion, appears with victorious arm aloft, turning, as* TOKIO, *also in*

*slow motion, climbs through imaginary ropes to
embrace him.* TOM *and* ROXY *appear to clap each
other on the back. Upstage, unseen by them,* LORNA
stands in a spot, gazing across at JOE; *she sings the
same fragment, not quite ready to say the words:*)

LORNA:

> I wanna—
> I wanna be with—

(ROXY *and* TOKIO *take* JOE *off;* TOM *joins* LORNA.)

TOM: Yeah, he's boxing beautiful, wings on those gloves,
but what's inside, canary birds? The kid has no
punch!

LORNA: I've seen him punch.

TOM: You've got good eyes. You'd think a fresh ugly
brat like that could hit out—

LORNA: Joe's a very nice-looking boy. You never looked.

TOM [AMUSED]: What, that jig? We get off this tour I'm
gonna have your eyes examined!

(TOM *kisses her cheek, and leaves;* LORNA *stands
alone, grim. A corner of a gym moves in, and* JOE
entering to pack a small bag sees her; LORNA *with
a nod starts off.*)

JOE: Lorna.

(*She halts; he is hesitant.*)

Miss Moon. Mr. Gottlieb, I don't know what to
call you—

LORNA [SMILES]: My momma called me Lorna, you're
no better.

JOE: Haven't we met somewhere? I mean, training and
fighting and travelling and training, all I see of you
is—your other half.

LORNA [WRYLY]: Well. If you want an easy life you have
to expect to work—

(She turns, to evade this encounter.)

JOE: No. I expect more.

(His voice is harder, and it stops her.)

Lorna, I expected more.

LORNA [PAUSE]: All I want is peace and quiet, Joe. At
twenty you want to discover America and at thirty
your feet hurt, I just want to sleep my days out like
a tired cat—

*(TOM and ROXY walk in to join JOE; opposite, EDDIE
SATIN appears with a henchman.)*

TOM: Joe, let me talk to you like a poppa. Now you're as
pretty a picture fighter as anyone's seen—

ROXY: Only who buys pictures?

TOM: Right. Stop saving yourself, the big money is in the
big punch, the kayo—

JOE [DRY]: You don't sound like *my* poppa.

EDDIE [IMPERIOUS]: Joe Wellington.

(JOE turns; they appraise each other.)

Son, I'm Eddie Satin.

JOE: Yeah, I'm impressed.

TOM: What are you doing in Cleveland, Eddie?

EDDIE: I have contacts all over. Your boy can fight his way up there, Tom. I like to see boys of color win a title, I'm thinking of buying a piece of his contract—

TOM: No—

ROXY: Eddie, we got enough troubles!

TOM: We're not selling. Eddie, you got your hand in everything from whores to horse, let us make a nickel without you butting in!

EDDIE [QUIETLY]: Don't turn your back on me, Tom, you might find a knife in it.

(*An instant chill of silence.*)

TOM [PLACATING]: Eddie, all I mean is I don't know how Joe'll shape up in the next six months—

EDDIE: Let the kid decide.

JOE [FLAT]: I don't see any kids around here, just a few old goats.

(*He starts off.*)

EDDIE: Hear me out, Joe!

(JOE *halts to listen.*)

Money don't interest me, you take my share. I'll see you get Garden bouts, TV, top contenders—Lombardo, Fulton, Lopez—you write your own ticket to the top. Yes or no?

JOE [DELIBERATELY]: Mr. Satin. I gave it a try and I think the try is over.

(*He shakes his head.*)

I mean, what *is* this? I train like a dog, fight for ten
cents a week, live in dressing rooms where the stink
hits me worse than the bums Tom signs me to
fight, the crowds boo because I don't go into the
ring with an axe, and—

(*A glance at* LORNA:)

—nobody talks to me, except to say give more.
What for?

EDDIE: You're not managed right.

JOE: But if you buy in and I find a knife in *my* back I'll
be managed right? Thanks.

(*He turns again to leave, but* EDDIE's *gentle voice
wins his attention.*)

EDDIE: Joe. Soul brother. I'm a black man, dig me. In
your ear.

(*Arm around* JOE, *he walks him aside.*)

Use them like they use you. I do, and I live good.
Get with me, yes?

(JOE *hesitates.*)

No?

(JOE *hesitates;* EDDIE *smiles.*)

Maybe?

JOE [PAUSE]: Show me.
EDDIE: Be my guest.

(*His gesture invites* JOE *away from the others.*)

> *This is the life,*
> *Here's where the living is.*
> *This is the life,*
> *Baby, you're there.*
>
> *This is the life,*
> *You've waited long enough.*
> *Man, you've arrived.*
> *Breathe in that air!*
>
> *Wine and perfume,*
> *Silver and candlelight!*
> *Children, make way!*
> *Joe's here to stay!*
>
> *Come join the club,*
> *Hear that sweet music start.*
> *This is the life, sweetheart!*

(JOE *is not convinced, and turns back.*)

Don't be a square, Joe.

> *Tell them bye-bye,*
> *Get where the action is.*
> *Come have some fun,*
> *I'll lead the way.*

This is the life!
They've kept you in a box,
Break down the walls,
Come out and play!

See all the lights,
They're spelling Wellington!
How sweet the song
When you belong.

Top of the heap,
That's how it's gotta be.
This is the life—you'll see!

(The corner of the gym has moved out, and the other characters with it; now a sexy Negro girl dances in to circle JOE, and other dancers appear, a flashy and opulent group, who surround JOE and present him with some of the items named in the chant.)

JOE:

Can I be what I want to be?

EDDIE:

Yes, you can!

JOE:

Can I get what I want to get?

GROUP:

Yes, you can!

JOE:

Can I have a car
With a built-in bar?

GROUP:

> And a color TV
> And a Playboy key!

JOE:

> And a hundred shares
> Of AT&T?

EDDIE:

> Yes, you can!
> Yes, you can!

GROUP:

> And a contour chair,
> Imported booze—

JOE:

> Calendar watch,
> Custom-made shoes?

GROUP:

> Photograph in the Daily News!

EDDIE:

> Yes, you can!

GROUP:

> Uh huh!
> Ten-dollar ties,
> Yes sir, how many?
> You'll get to call Leonard Bernstein
>   Lenny!
> Lunch at Shor's,
> Pick up the tab!

JOE:

> Doorman saying,
> "Can I get you a cab?"

GROUP [WHISTLE]:

> Cab!

JOE:

> *Thank you!*

GROUP:

> *Air conditioned flat,*
> *Trip to France—*

JOE:

> *Rex Harrison hat*
> *And real tight pants!*

GIRL:

> *Oh well, your pants!*

JOE [TO HERS]:

> *No, those pants!*

GROUP:

> *Uh huh!*
> *Bartenders asking,*
> *"What'll you have?"*
> *Charge account*
> *At Saks Fifth Ave!*
> *Diamond studs,*
> *Finest grade—*

JOE:

> *Every single album*
> *Ray Charles ever made!*

(*They all dance,* JOE *with them.*)

GROUP:

> *Polaroid camera!*

JOE:

> *Stereo sets!*

GROUP:

> *Season box—*

JOE:

> To see the Mets!

GROUP:

> Charcoal grill—

JOE:

> With a Nathan's frank!

GROUP:

> Diners' Club card—

JOE:

> And money in the bank!

GROUP:

> Shave and a haircut—

JOE:

> Me next!

GROUP:

> This is the life,
> Here's where the living is.
> This is the life,
> Baby, you're there!

(JOE *concludes a solo dance with a cartwheel, and the group hoists him onto their shoulders.*)

10.

The marquee of Madison Square Garden descends, with
JOE's *name featured on it, and under it a dressing room*
slides in; the roar of the fight crowd is audible. TOKIO
takes JOE *behind a panel to change into fight togs.* TOM
and LORNA *enter at one side, and* EDDIE *and* ROXY *at the*
other; EDDIE *now dominates them all.*

EDDIE: Tom.

> (*He gives him some legal papers.*)

The new contract. I'm in for thirty per cent, my
check's enclosed—
TOM [EXPOSTULATING]: Thirty—
EDDIE: Don't mention it, just sign it.
LORNA [STARING UP AT THE MARQUEE]: You really got
him in—
EDDIE: Little influence in the wrong circles never hurt
anyone.
ROXY [TO JOE BEHIND PANEL]: Joe, I gotta give the devil
his dues: the past six months you done a okay job.
EDDIE: Okay isn't good enough.
ROXY [FLUSTERED]: Yeah, okay isn't good enough!

JOE [EMERGES]: Thanks, Roxy.

EDDIE: Joe, you're in the Garden now—

ROXY: —on nationwide TV—

EDDIE: —but this racket is a penny candy store today, anything less'n a big-draw champ is still nothing. This crowd is here for one thing, blood. Draw me some blood, Joe!

TOM: He means slug!

EDDIE [STARTS OFF]: Draw me blood tonight and I'll really show you the world.

TOKIO: Okay, let's go.

(*The men move off.* JOE *is following, past* LORNA, *when her words—they are almost to herself— catch him.*)

LORNA: I don't want you to win now, Joe.

JOE: What?

LORNA [SHAKES HER HEAD]: Nothing. Good luck.

(*She starts out.*)

JOE: Lorna!

(*He takes a step after her.*)

I'm moving up, move with me—

LORNA: Don't devil me, Joe. I'm an old lady, soon I'll be a married old lady—

JOE: You told me pick a diamond—

LORNA [PAUSE]: You picked him. Eddie Satin. Just be careful who wears who.

JOE: I can think of a worse guy in this dressing room.

LORNA [SHARPLY]: You're wrong.

(*She turns away;* FRANK, *unseen by either, enters at a distance in time to hear* JOE's *cry:*)

JOE: Outcast to outcast, tell me straight, you *love* that red-headed hater? And if you do—what's that make you, Miss Moon?
LORNA [FLATLY]: Mrs. Moody.
JOE: And if you don't, it makes you Mrs. sleep your days out with the man with a buck!

(*He raises his fists in a rage, incredulous:*)

Which *these* put in his pocket? I hope you both drown in it!
LORNA [FLARING]: Well, you're a one to talk! Who said he wanted in—who said—
JOE: This isn't all I wanted! You think I fight just for money and that mob of hyenas? I also fight for you, Miss Lorna Moon!

(*A pause; then* LORNA *speaks levelly, laying it on the line:*)

LORNA: What are you offering, Joe?—a walk hand in hand down the street with half the world biting at me every step—

(TOKIO *runs back in.*)

TOKIO: Joe!
JOE [FURIOUS]: I'm offering *me*!

(TOKIO *puts an arm around him, to hustle him out.*)

I am what I am—

(TOKIO *turns him,* JOE *throws him off.*)

If you don't want me I know who does! You'll see
me wear a crown, Mrs. Moody! You'll see me wear
a *crown*—

(TOKIO *swings and thrusts him out; the roar of the
crowd mounts.*)

FRANK: In here, Pop.

(WELLINGTON *enters behind* FRANK, *as* LORNA *wheels
to see them.*)

LORNA: Poppa Wellington—
WELLINGTON: Miss Moon. My Joe ain't here?
LORNA: He's in the ring. Hurry and you'll see the fight—
this way—
WELLINGTON [NOT MOVING]: Joe sent us a pass, I saw the
others. I don't wanna see Joe get hit.
FRANK [WITH A CERTAIN WEIGHT]: In the ring or out,
Miss Moon.
WELLINGTON: My boy Frank.

(FRANK *moves in.*)

FRANK: I'll tell you something about my brother, Miss
Moon, he's nobody's brother.
LORNA: What?

FRANK: He thinks if he's famous he'll be everybody's. Is
that what you think?

(*He appraises her.*)

It's why Joe wants all the riches of this world.

LORNA: Who doesn't, is that wrong?
FRANK: It's *hard*. Because it's your world.
LORNA: Who died and left me the world? Don't put it
on my back—
FRANK: Miss Moon, here's the truth—if Joe can't make
your world, and can't live in ours, he's a man falling
in space. Now think twice and think deep—

(*The roar of the crowd leaps abruptly to an uncon-
tainable paroxysm of excitement.*)

WELLINGTON: What's happening?
LORNA [STRICKEN]: Somebody's hurt—
WELLINGTON: Joe?

(LORNA *runs out;* FRANK, *after a look at his father,
runs after her.* WELLINGTON *stands alone, trembling,
and lets out a cry of fear:*)

Joe!

(*But* LORNA *and* FRANK *are swept back in by a tide
of followers behind and around* JOE; *it fans out in
a semicircle, with* JOE *in its center between his
father and* LORNA, *both downstage. The dialogue*

comes pell-mell, the followers slapping each other on the back, but every word conveying the news of a knockout must be audible.)

EDDIE: Joe, you did it for me!
ROXY: A knockout! A knockout!
TOM: Get the sports writers in!
TOKIO: Knocks him out in one round!
EDDIE: One minute!
TOM: One punch!
ROXY: All my faith and patience is rewarded!
EDDIE: Joe, you're a golden boy!

(But WELLINGTON makes worriedly for JOE, and grabs his right hand in both his own to stare into his bleeding face; JOE doubling up in pain twists away. A tremolo commences in the orchestra, all onstage instantly hushed, and JOE, face to face with LORNA, grins at her.)

TOKIO: What's the matter, Joe?
JOE [EYES ON LORNA]: Better cut it off.
TOKIO: Hurt?
JOE: It's broken.

(TOKIO with a scissors cuts the glove in an utter silence; but as he works JOE begins to laugh, softly, then louder, and when TOKIO removes the glove JOE thrusts the bared hand aloft in victory.)

I just got baptized!

(Now EDDIE *runs in to hug him, and all—except for* FRANK, WELLINGTON, *and* LORNA—*throng around him in jubilation.*)

EDDIE:

> *See the boy*
> *Who's gonna fight now—*

JOE: The boy has a profession!

ALL:

> *See the boy*
> *Start moving right now—*

JOE: It's the beginning of the kingdom!

ALL:

> *Stick around, baby,*
> *And see!*

Curtain.

ACT TWO

1.

A bar. LORNA *is seated drinking at it, alone, except for the bartender.*

LORNA:

> You're the boy
> Who wanted everything.
> Golden boy,
> There's no golden ring.
>
> The things you need
> You need too much,
> The love you feel
> You feel too much,
> So when you're hurt
> It hurts too much—
> I know. . . .
>
> Golden boy,
> You think you need me so,
> Little boy,
> Too naïve to know
>
> Weary girls like me
> Have nothing left,

So how could we
Give something to
Golden boys like you?

Is it all too late,
Or could I find
The strength somewhere
To see it through
With a boy
Like you?

(TOM *enters, to watch her; he is troubled.*)

TOM: Honey, why do you drink like that?

LORNA: There's a—lump I drink to dissolve, baby, do you mind?

TOM: Don't drink alone. Give me a double.

(*The bartender serves him.*)

You get a fighter like Joe once in a lifetime, and he's slipping through my fingers.

(LORNA *sits looking into her glass, not at him.* TOM *hits the bar.*)

Goddamit! They gang up, it's a race war. I got no civil rights?

LORNA [DRAWLS]: Fight for them, baby.

TOM: Yeah. Fight Eddie and float down the river—

LORNA: Demonstrate.

TOM [SITS BESIDE HER]: One thing, Monica's going to Reno this month.

LORNA: Reno, pardner, that sure is the most helluva hard town to find.

(FRANK *walks in, looking around; his head is band-aged.*)

FRANK: Afternoon, friends. They said look here.

(LORNA *turns; it is* JOE's *brother, and her eyes are bright on him throughout.*)

LORNA: The spirit of '76. What did you do, run into a law?

FRANK [SMILES]: Yes, I— Well, we might say stars fell on Alabama. Here.

(*He gives* TOM *a roll of money.*)

My father doesn't want this money. Joe sent it to him.

LORNA [IRONIC]: He remembers his folks?

FRANK: More or less. More with money, less with—

(*His gesture evokes the heart.*)

What is it, a man puts on a gold watch, he forgets the time of year, hm? Joe had a birthday, we didn't see him.

LORNA: Don't look at me, I wouldn't know him if he said hello to me.

TOM: Hell, he won't give us the time of day.

FRANK [WRY]: Maybe his watch stopped.

(To LORNA, *mildly pointed:*)

I mean between Harlem and here—

(*He nods, starts out.*)

TOM: You got a better build than Joe, ever think of
     fighting?
FRANK [SMILES]: I fight.
TOM: Yeah, but what do you get for it? A busted head—
FRANK: I get what Joe doesn't.

(*After a moment he walks out.*)

LORNA [INTO HER GLASS]: Say hello for me—
TOM [SUDDENLY]: Help me, Lorna.

(LORNA *goes motionless.*)

LORNA [THEN]: How?
TOM: Get to Joe.
LORNA: How?
TOM: Get to him. Steer him away from selling me out—
LORNA: You want me to—
TOM: —he used to listen to you— I need a year, I can't
     save a dollar with the alimony—
LORNA [VERY QUIET]: Don't send me, Tom.
TOM: I've got to hang on till he wins the crown!
LORNA [TREMBLING]: Don't—send me—

(EDDIE SATIN *saunters in, with a manila envelope;
his manner is curt.*)

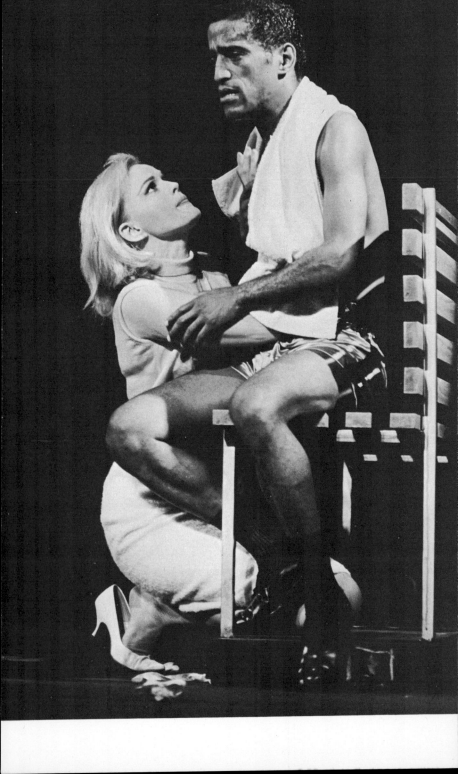

EDDIE: Nobody in the office, everyone a bar fly. White folks, look out for the swatter.

(*He tosses the envelope on the bar.*)

New pictures of Joe, use them, Tom, I like them better. I also like your phone to answer if Joe calls. What do you figure your interest in him is worth?

(TOM *freezes, with the photos out.*)

TOM: Why?

EDDIE: I'm thinking of handling him myself. Fifteen grand?

(*He slides a photo towards the bartender.*)

Tell Maxie I'd like it in the window. Seventeen five?

TOM [RISES]: You've got a gall. That boy is worth ten times that—

EDDIE: Don't talk back, Tom, I'll send my lawyers before I sign Joe to meet Lopez.

(*He is on his way out when* TOM *bends urgently to* LORNA, *who is gazing at one of the photos.*)

TOM [LOW]: Lorna—talk to him—

(EDDIE *wheels, stares;* TOM *under his eye walks unsteadily out of the bar.* EDDIE *comes to contemplate the photo in* LORNA's *hand.*)

EDDIE: A beauty—a trim and genuine black beauty—

(LORNA *puts the photo down, rises, and walks out
as the lights fade on the bar moving off.*)

2.

EDDIE's *penthouse apartment gathers around him where he stands; a party is in full swing, with a wide variety of guests, Negro and white, from beatniks to those in full evening dress. LORNA, TOM, and ROXY are soon present.*

EDDIE:

> *While the city sleeps,*
> *While the streets are clear,*
> *There's a life that's happening here.*
>
> *While the tourist dreams*
> *In his Statler bed,*
> *Here we're living those dreams instead.*
>
> *Hey, the clan has gathered!*
> *Put a Stan Getz record on,*
> *Send the judge for pizza,*
> *When the last anchovy's gone,*
> *Then it's dawn.*
>
> *While the city sleeps,*
> *When the air is still,*

Life can bring you that secret thrill!
While the city sleeps,
While the city sleeps.

When the Scarsdale squares
All have said their prayers,
We receive what they're praying for.

Well, the juice is flowing!
Hear those jungle drums begin,
Bossa nova going—
Hey, your Lordship, where you been?
Stagger in!

While the city sleeps,
When the air is still,
Life can bring you that secret thrill!
While the city sleeps,
While the city sleeps,
While the city sleeps.

(EDDIE *mingles with his guests.* LOPEZ, *a Puerto Rican fighter, enters on the landing, stands.*)

GIRL: Hey, Lopez is here!

(LOPEZ *crosses to a Negro couple, and the three dance in a contest of the two men for the girl; she chooses* LOPEZ. ROXY *calls—much of the dialogue is over other people's heads—to* EDDIE.)

ROXY: You run quite a joint here, Eddie. It was nothing like this at my bar-mitzvah!

EDDIE [THE PERFECT HOST]: Eat, drink, be merry.

(TOM *prowling avoids* EDDIE, *comes behind* LORNA.)

TOM: Yeah, tomorrow we die. You find Joe?

(*She shakes her head.*)

EDDIE: Joe's out on the Thruway.
ROXY: Doing what?
EDDIE [JUDICIOUS]: About a hundred and ten.
TOM: What?
EDDIE: Fighter of the month, I gave him a new Ferrari.
TOM: A Ferrari—
ROXY: He can kill himself in a car like that!
TOM [GLOOMY]: Our boy is living fast—
EDDIE [EASILY]: Go rub against some of the girls, part-
    ners, your edges are square.

(*He drifts off, as a swankily dressed* JOE *and a
couple of devotees, including a Negro beauty, come
in on the landing;* JOE *tosses and catches the car
keys, and shouts across the room.*)

JOE: Eddie, it's a beauty! You manage me right!
TOM [URGENT]: Honey, talk to him soon, huh?

(LORNA *is unresponsive, her eyes on* JOE.)

ROXY: Joe, a Ferrari does a hundred and fifty, I don't
    want my investment wrapped around a telephone
    pole—
EDDIE [PLEASANTLY]: What investment?

JOE: Afraid I might enjoy life, Roxy?
TOM [APPROACHING]: Joe, you know we have your good
    at heart—
JOE: Prove it. Get me the Lopez fight—

(*Witheringly:*)

—Uncle Tom.

TOM [CONTROLLING HIMSELF]: You have a big mouth—
JOE [SHOUTS]: Eddie! I want Lopez next!
EDDIE [SHOUTS BACK]: You have him!
JOE: Don't worry about cars, Tom, worry where you fit
    in this syndicate.

(EDDIE *escorts* LOPEZ *through the party, to* JOE.)

EDDIE: Pepe Lopez, numero uno.

(LOPEZ *offers his hand; instead* JOE *feints him, a
quick mock-combination, and* LOPEZ *leaps back,
startled; he unleashes a prolonged torrent of angry
Spanish, and stalks out of the party in a huff.* JOE
calls after him:)

JOE: Same to you, baby, in colored!
TOM [TO LORNA]: Will you talk to him, for God sakes?
LORNA: Yes.

(TOM *makes himself scarce in the party. A* REPORTER
with a notebook nabs JOE.)

REPORTER: What will you do against Lopez?

JOE [CURT]: Win.

REPORTER: Name the round?

JOE: One.

(JOE *turns away, and finds himself for the first time* *confronting* LORNA; *he stops.*)

REPORTER [WRITING]: Son, you make colorful copy.

(JOE *eyes* LORNA, *then grins, and from her turns* *back to the* REPORTER; *the song he delivers at him* *is aimed at her.*)

JOE: Daddy, you don' know how colorful Ah been.

When I was very young,
Brand new upon the scene,
Had no experience,
That's right—I was green!

Then I grew up a bit,
Found out a thing or two,
Sometimes I'd get unhappy,
In short—I was blue!

As far as politics go, I never turned red,
I'm smarter than you might think.
And every time I've been told,
"Boy, you're good as gold,"
Say, I'm just tickled pink!

I've tried all sorts of shades,
Put them all to the test.

But I look at myself,
And black—suits me best!

Black is chic,
Always correct for the house or yard.
Black is neat,
Goes with everything, and doesn't try too hard.
Black is basic, you'll agree.
As the Duchess of Windsor would say,
"Black is me!"

Well, I've been yellow at times, I'm sorry to say,
Yes, I've been afraid to fight.
Sure, I've been scared as can be,
But take it from me,
I never quite turned white!

And when I'm old and gray,
Heading for my last rest,
Guess I'll still have to say
That black—
Not Kelly green,
Black—
Not tangerine,
Black—
That's B-L-A-C-K— Dig?
Black
Suits me best!

(When JOE turns away from the song, LORNA is
waiting for him; they gaze at each other.)

LORNA [THEN]: What color is the Ferrari?

JOE: Gray.

LORNA [NODS]: Suits me best. Will you give the lady a ride?

JOE [STARES]: You're putting me on.

LORNA: I want to talk, Joe.

JOE [PAUSE]: I want to listen.

(He indicates the landing with a hand; she hurries past him, and JOE follows her. TOM comes center to stare after them, as the lights dim, the penthouse disappears, and the guests melt away.)

3.

JOE *and* LORNA *walk, not together, as a river-and-bridge scene with a bench forms around them; it is night.*

JOE [IMPATIENT]: What do I need him for?

LORNA: All he asks is a year, Joe. He's poor compared to you. You're alive, you've got yourself, you're a— man, he's a desperate kid at forty-two—

JOE [FLAT]: Tom's feelings don't interest me.

LORNA: Mine do, Joe. Tell the truth.

JOE: Then talk about you.

LORNA: I'm sorry for him. You and I are what he has, period, and what I—

(She sits on the bench, averted from him.)

Joe, there's been a lot of men, went through me like —traffic in the tunnel, and the twice I was in love I took an awful beating, and he—what he did—was pick me out of my filth, and wash my face and comb my— And once I tried to leave him, he drank some—

(She is weeping.)

—misery reached out to misery—Joe dear, you know
that, in your own heart I *know* you know that—
JOE [PAUSE]: I'll call Eddie off.

(*He turns away, to the river.*)

Oh Christ, white or black, why's it so hard?
LORNA: Thank you, Joe.

(*She rises to leave.*)

I know everything that's wrong with him—because
he loves me and I'm rotten, when somebody loves
me I ask myself what's wrong with *them*—
JOE [GRIMLY]: What's wrong with me?

(*He turns to face her.*)

Lorna, I'm on my feet, I don't *need* you, but every
time you come around it's a promise, you never kept
that promise—
LORNA [VERY STILL]: I know, Joe—
JOE: But you don't know how *I* feel? Lorna, when I'm
not with you I—*bleed*, I got a hole bleeding in my
side nothing can stop but being with you because
the other **half** is you, rotten, beautiful, the other
half is you!—and I'm here on my feet, bleeding—
for you—

(*His hand is out for her. Slowly she comes to it,
black and white hands clasp, and the song begins.*)

Lorna—
Lorna and Joe—

Somehow it sounds so right—
Somehow you feel what I feel too—

I wanna be with you,
I wanna be with you,
I wanna be with you!

After all the nights of wanting you,
Lying there, loving you, hating you,
Tonight I'm touching you, tasting you!
World, you're gonna see,
We'll make out somehow.
Here's my girl and me,
They can't hurt us now.

We're gonna have it all,
I'll love you every day,
Honey, life could be so great for us,
Here's our chance, it's not too late for us,
Grab it fast or life won't wait for us!

I wanna be with you,
I wanna be with you—

LORNA [THEN]: Joe, darling, I'll—tell Tom—
JOE: When?
LORNA: Not tonight.
JOE: Quick, do it quick.
LORNA: Tomorrow. Not tonight.
JOE: Lorna—

(Now *it hits him, he spins around with the ecstasy of it.*)

Lorna, what color, what color am I? No—*color!*

LORNA:

> *You make me want to sing!*
> *You make me want to cry!*
>
> *Joe, I didn't want to feel again,*
> *But here I am, scared again, real again.*
> *I wanna be with you,*
> *Stay with you,*
> *With you every day—*

JOE:

> *Lorna—*

LORNA:

> *With you right or wrong—*

JOE:

> *Lorna—*

LORNA:

> *With you every way—*

JOE:

> *I will be so good to you—*

LORNA:

> *With you I am strong—*

JOE:

> *I still can't believe it's true—*

LORNA:

> *That's how it's gonna be—*

JOE:

> *That's how it's gonna be,*
> *My loving girl and me—*

BOTH:

> *And we'll tell the world make way for us,*
> *It's a sweet and golden day for us,*

Now the music starts to play for us!
I wanna be with you!

(LORNA *stands trembling.*)

LORNA: Joe, take me somewhere, take me somewhere—
Oh my God, I'll fall all apart if you—don't hold
me—

(JOE *comes to take her face in his hands, and kisses
her on the mouth, gently; the warmth of mouth to
mouth steals over their bodies, their arms slowly
enveloping each in the other's, until they are one
figure, totally joined. The lights dim out on them.*)

4.

Dawn in the park. JOE enters, walking almost on air, and does a softshoe dance as he sings:

JOE:

> Can't you see it?
> It's clear as it can be!
> It makes a sunny beam of light
> That seems to follow me.
>
> Can't you hear it?
> Sopranos everywhere!
> A chorus of the choicest voices
> Trilling in the air.
>
> It makes the soot
> Underfoot
> Flash like diamonds,
> And every cop
> Dances by
> Like Fred Astaire!
>
> Can't you see it?
> It's splashed across the sky.

If you can see it,
You're as happy as I.

Can't you feel it?
It's pleasanter than spring.
It's like the humble peasant felt
The day they made him king.

It makes those fumes
From the bus
Smell delicious,
And every bum
On a bench
Sings just like Bing!

Can't you see it?
It makes the buildings fly.
If you can see it,
You're as happy as I!

(He dances off.)

5.

___

TOM's *office.* LORNA *is in it alone, sunk in a chair, sunk in herself, thinking of* JOE, *profoundly depressed, moveless.* TOM *comes in, drying his hands with a paper towel.*

TOM: You're late, honey.

LORNA [FROM THE GRAVE]: The late—Miss Moon.

TOM: Penny for your thoughts.

LORNA: Joe.

TOM: What did he say?

LORNA [WITH AN EFFORT]: Said okay.

TOM [SIGHS]: That's a relief—

LORNA [TO HERSELF, MORDANT]: Why don't I live my life out in this chair? It's got arms—

TOM [NOT HEARING]: It's a wedding present, honey, you ready to change your name?

(LORNA *shakes her head, heavy as the dead, and whispers, not to him:*)

LORNA: I can't—change anything, I'm tired, old, don't want any new—worlds, can't take another—step, I'm so—

(*She is shaken, covers her eyes, shutting it out.*)

—scared—I can't *change*, no—

TOM [IN WONDER]: Honey, I'm an old shoe, remember?

(*He comes to kiss her nape, and she is out of the chair like a shot; at the desk she sees the roll of money.*)

LORNA: You haven't the sense of a halfwit!

TOM: What?

LORNA: Leave that money on the desk with the door open, anyone can walk away with it! It belongs to Joe.

TOM [PUZZLED]: I'll give it to him—

(LORNA *finds herself confronting a wallful of prize-fighter photos, veers away in a bitter outburst:*)

LORNA: Spent half my life in this damned office, like a jail, I could scream for help. When did you last say something new to me?

TOM: Lorna, I don't know what the—

LORNA: When did you last look at me?

TOM: What are we fighting about?

LORNA [WITH LOATHING FOR THE WORD]: Love. Love, I'm trying to tell you love doesn't *last*—

TOM: It does for us.

LORNA: Not for us, not for—anybody, I've been through that lie too often even when it was simple—

TOM: I need it to last. I know what I need, I need you.

LORNA: —wake up and it's all a dream, nothing there, nothing lasts, it has to end—

TOM: What has to end?

LORNA: Everything.

TOM: What everything?

LORNA [MISERABLE]: I want to—

(*She cannot look at him, and is hardly audible.*)

—leave you, Tom.

TOM [A SICK SMILE]: That's what you think. I'd cut my throat.

LORNA: I mean it.

TOM: I mean it too.

LORNA [STARES AT HIM]: You'd—do it—

(*And it is a visible relief to her.* TOM *can say nothing, but stares back.*)

You're pale—

(*She touches his cheek, walks around.*)

Put that money somewhere, it makes me nervous—

TOM: Who's the man?

(LORNA *shakes her head, and he suddenly embraces her.* JOE *appears in the doorway,* EDDIE *behind him, and halts.* LORNA *breaks away.*)

JOE [LONG PAUSE]: The last farewell.

EDDIE [SARDONIC]: Partner. I changed my mind.

TOM [EYES ON LORNA]: About what?

EDDIE: The contract. I made the Lopez deal today, they meet six weeks from tonight—

JOE [REACHES FOR HER ARM, GENTLY]: All right, Lorna,
  beat it.

TOM: What?

JOE: She's not coming here again.

(TOM *glares at him, the enmity of months ready to
erupt.*)

TOM: Whyn't you mind your own goddam business?

JOE [SOFTLY]: What else *is* my goddam business, Tom?

TOM: Your business is take orders, you take orders from
  me—

JOE: Who are you, God? I don't want her in here
  again—

TOM [OVERLAPPING]: Yes, you snotty rat, I'm *your*
  maker! You did me such a favor? Son of a bitch,
  get your nose out!

EDDIE [QUIETLY]: He's your best friend, Tom—

TOM [TURNING]: I wouldn't take the crap of this last year
  from the President. You want to manage this boy?
  —help yourself! I'll sell my piece for whatever, thirty
  grand and let me out! Twenty, I'll take twenty, I
  got my girl, I don't need a million, I take my girl
  and it's everything.

JOE [SCOWLING]: What girl?

TOM: I don't talk to you.

(To EDDIE:)

Well?

EDDIE: I do what Joe wants, Tom.

JOE [WHEELS]: You didn't tell him?

LORNA [WRETCHED]: Joe, don't—
TOM: Tell him what?
JOE: I'll tell him. Listen to me—
LORNA: Joe, I *beg* you—
TOM: What goes on, what the hell—
JOE: Listen to me! Lorna loves me.

(TOM *looks from one to the other, takes a step back.*)

TOM: You—

(*He is unbelieving.*)

You crazy—black—bastard—
JOE [TREMBLING]: Tell him, Lorna.
LORNA [PAUSE, AVERTED]: I love Tom. Tell him what?

(JOE *incredulously spins her around to stare in her face, and* TOM *comes at him swinging.* JOE *ducks, grabs* TOM *by the throat with his left and backs him against the desk, his right fist cocked, trembling to let it fly and barely controlling it when he hears* LORNA *scream:*)

I beg you!

(JOE *releases* TOM, *who staggers away to get his breath.*)

TOM: What—what—went on—between you—

(LORNA's *eyes are only on* JOE, *and his on hers; his
voice, when at last he can use it, is deadly as dry
ice.*)

JOE: Nothing—nothing—nothing between us—nothing
is between us.

(*Turning, he walks out of the office, stands in the
darkness.*)

EDDIE [VERY OMINOUS]: Don't you like living, Tom? I
don't want you to call our boy that again.

(*He follows* JOE. TOM's *eyes are on* LORNA, *bent over
the chair in her own agony, as the lights dim.*)

6.

——

The office gives way to the Harlem street, forming around JOE, *the inhabitants wandering in; it is 127th Street, but by night, and the mood quite transformed.* JOE *begins a song as if to* LORNA:

JOE:

> I gave you my soul:
> Well, no more.
> Now I'll kiss your eyes
> No more.
> How I trusted you!
> Now I ask—what for?
> You were life to me,
> But no more.
>
> Well, you had your chance.
> No more.
> Now I'll play the fool
> No more.
> How I needed love!
> But you closed the door.
> Oh, you'll laugh at me
> No more.

(The others take up the same song, alternating passages with JOE; *but he is singing a private lament, they are singing a public resolve.)*

ALL:

How I bled for you!
No more.
Shed my skin for you.
No more.
Oh, I worshipped you,
That you can't ignore.
But I ain't your slave
No more.

Well, you had your way!
No more!
Well, it ain't your day
No more!
Well, I'm standin' up,
I ain't on the floor.
I ain't bowin' down
No more!
I ain't gonna cry
No more!
I ain't gonna cry
No more!
No more!

JOE:

I just wanted love,
Why'd it turn to war? . . .

ALL:

> I *ain't bowin' down,*
> I *ain't bowin' down,*
> I *ain't bowin' down,*
> *No more!*

(*The group goes into a dance, strong, defiant, but it does not include* JOE; *he wanders among them as only a spectator of their solidarity, and though time after time a dancer extends a hand to invite him in, he is unclaimed by their movement as a mass group. It comes to its climax without him, and he leaves on a personal utterance—"I ain't your slave" —while they close on the social one in unison, "I ain't bowin' down no more."*

The Harlem street disappears.)

7.

The dressing-room moves in, with a distant roar of voices
under the scene. TOKIO is working at a locker, ROXY hanging around, with WELLINGTON, ANNA, and RONNIE waiting
on a bench opposite.

RONNIE [INDICATING IT]: The roar of the crowd, folks—
ANNA: Must be a thousand people.
RONNIE: Six thousand.
ROXY: Nine thousand, mostly goyem. We're sitting
    under them.
RONNIE [ALARMED]: Suppose they fell down on my wife's
    hat?

(EDDIE comes in, glances around.)

EDDIE: Where's Joe?
TOKIO: Upstairs with the sports writers.
EDDIE [INCREDULOUS]: A half hour before a fight? Go up
    and get him.

(TOKIO and ROXY leave; EDDIE stares at the others.)

Who are you?

WELLINGTON: I'm Joe's poppa.
RONNIE: I'm Joe's poppa's son-in-law—
EDDIE: Joe invited you?

(WELLINGTON *shakes his head, and* EDDIE *goes cold.*)

He's fighting a good man tonight, when he goes in
there with Lopez I like him to have one thing on
his mind, fighting. Don't be here when I get back.

(*He walks out.*)

ANNA: That's a positive personality!
RONNIE [ON HIS WAY]: Come on, folks—
WELLINGTON: I'm gonna wait for Joe.
RONNIE: You wanna miss the whole card?
WELLINGTON: I'm gonna wait.
ANNA: Poppa, you heard what the man said—
WELLINGTON: I'm gonna wait for Joe!

(RONNIE *hesitates, then hands* WELLINGTON *a ticket.*)

RONNIE: See that number? It's for identifyin' the body!

(*He leaves with* ANNA, *as* LORNA *enters opposite en
route to the lockers;* WELLINGTON *gets up, and*
LORNA's *step falters as she sees him.*)

LORNA: Poppa Wellington. What brings you down here?
WELLINGTON: I come to see my Joe.
LORNA: Is anything wrong?
WELLINGTON: He don' come to see me. I miss him.
LORNA: Oh Lord, is anything right—

(JOE *in a fight robe comes striding in; he stops to stare at them together.*)

WELLINGTON: Joe—
JOE: Poppa, your age, you messing around with these ofay chicks?

(*To* LORNA:)

What are you doing in here?
LORNA: Looking for—scissors—
JOE: Who're you cutting up today?
LORNA: Items—for the press book—

(*She finds scissors, sits on the bench, and begins to clip.* JOE *yanks the newspapers out of her hand.*)

JOE: When I'm here you look me in the eye! You think I'm a ticket stub, the show's over, throw me away? Poppa, wait outside.

(LORNA *tries to look him in the eye, but cannot, and she sits before the executioner, head bowed for the axe.* WELLINGTON *looks from one to the other and plods out, to wait on steps outside the dressing room, but in light and within earshot.*)

What's it like in bed with him?

(LORNA *shakes her bowed head.*)

Zero. Lorna, why, why, why, why, why?
LORNA: He—needs me—

JOE: I need you. Tell the truth!

LORNA [AT LAST]: I haven't—the guts to—make a life—with you.

JOE: You said to me—you said to me I'll fall apart if you don't hold me, and my God how I held you—

(*He is desperate, but almost tender.*)

—what do you say to him?

(LORNA *shakes her head.*)

No, tell me, you owe me a sentence—

LORNA [FAINT]: I say—move over in the—coffin, make room for me.

(JOE *is sick for her too, and is raising a hand to her in compassion when* TOM, ROXY, TOKIO, *and* EDDIE *with a package enter; instead he turns, waving* LORNA *out.*)

JOE: Get the girls out of here, it's not a hotel bedroom—

TOM: That's no way to talk!

JOE: I talk how I please!

TOM: Not to my wife, you don't!

(JOE *goes limp; he never quite comes out of this limpness before the fight.*)

JOE: Today? Oh Christ, that's perfect, the mating of zero and zero—

(*He sits averted against the rubdown table.*)

EDDIE [SAVAGE]: Get her out, Tom!

(TOM *starts out, but returns in anger for a last word with* JOE.)

TOM: I've got just one wish, for Lopez to give you the business, I hope he tears your head off—

EDDIE [FURIOUS]: What the hell are you up to tonight, ruin this boy?

(*He shoves* TOM, *who takes* LORNA *stumbling out,* ROXY *with them,* TOM *shouting back:*)

TOM: I'm versus you! Completely versus—

(EDDIE, *looking at* JOE *as he lies on his belly for* TOKIO'S *rubdown, is anxious to soothe him; he moves for his package.*)

EDDIE [GRIM]: I'll take that mother off the census list someday. Clear your mind of her, Joe. I got a present for you, you like this figure?

(*He dangles a white shirt in front of* JOE'S *eyes.*)

Silk, from Sulka's. I bought you a dozen. Ties—

(*He dangles a black tie on the shirt, and* JOE *notes it.*)

JOE: That color scheme'll never sell.

(*He rolls over, addresses the ceiling.*)

Eddie, I'm underdog three to two, what if I lose?

EDDIE: You're not a loser, baby.

JOE: You going to bring me silk shirts?

EDDIE [UNRUFFLED]: I *picked* my boy. I got forty thousand spread out tonight, you're going to the top. Lopez can't stop you and *you* can't stop you. You're not that kid in the dirty sneakers two years ago, you wear the best now, eat the best, sleep the best, and what did it?—one thing.

JOE: A good woman's love—

EDDIE: A killer's heart, sweet boy, I watched it come. You don't mess around in there now, you go for the kill, you got a real black beauty heart—right here—

(*And he lays his palm upon* JOE's *heart, and very gently massages it.* JOE *lies rigid.*)

JOE: Don't touch me.

(EDDIE *removes his hand;* JOE *rolls over on an elbow.*)

Eddie, I like girls.

EDDIE [UNEVENLY]: I gave you girls. I gave you everything you asked for—

JOE: You gave me *shit!*

EDDIE [BREATHING]: You asked for it. Joe baby, everything you got you asked for, if you don't like what you asked for you don't like you. Now don't get fancy on me, nigger, I keep my deals, you keep yours. I want Lopez taken out but good! You let *me* down the slab is waiting for your carcass!

(*He hits the rubdown table, and stalks out.* WELL-

INGTON *turns into the dressing room, and* JOE *glaring after* EDDIE *sees him;* JOE *lies down on his arms.)*

JOE: How's the family?
WELLINGTON: Fine, Joe.
JOE: Watch the fights on TV?
WELLINGTON: Ronnie do.
JOE [NOT LOOKING]: You look okay.
WELLINGTON: I don' feel so okay, Joe.
JOE: Why'd you send that money back?

(WELLINGTON *is silent;* JOE *shoots him a look.)*

You come to be my conscience, spit it out and beat it.
WELLINGTON: No. I come to see you, Joe. See how you makin' out. See why you wanna fight—

(JOE *puts his face down into his forearms, and his voice is muffled, long ago and far away.)*

JOE: Poppa, they were calling my name—they were calling my name—
WELLINGTON [LONG PAUSE]: Yeah. You fight. Too late not to fight, Joe, a man's gotta be happy not to fight. Now I see what you gotta do I give you every word to fight. Joe, I'm—sorry for you—
TOKIO [GENTLY]: I'll have to ask you to leave, Mr. W.
WELLINGTON: Joe. I hope you—win every fight.

(*He goes out heavily;* JOE's *face is still hidden in his forearms.)*

TOKIO: Coupla minutes to tune you up—
JOE: Tune me up. Tune me up.

(TOKIO *works, humming, then sings a fragment:*)

TOKIO:

>*—your head start achin'*
>*Makes your eyes unclear.*
>*Makes you waste your money,*
>*Turns you blind and dumb—*

(And JOE *begins to cry in his arms. When the buzzer sounds imperiously for the fight he shakes his head no in his arms, and* TOKIO *has to help him off the table; robe over his shoulders,* JOE *goes limply off with* TOKIO *in the dimming of lights.*)

8.

As the dressing-room disappears, stagehands run on and assemble the ring around an announcer talking into an overhead microphone through the roar of the crowd.

ANNOUNCER: Ladies and gentlemen, main event, ten rounds of boxing, winner to meet the lightweight champion of the world. In this corner, weighing a hundred and thirty-three and three-quarter pounds, in blue and gold trunks, the pride of Puerto Rico, unbeaten in twenty-two bouts, Pepe Lopez!

(LOPEZ enters his corner, full of bounce; his handlers attend him.)

And his opponent, in this corner, weighing one hundred thirty-three pounds, wearing black and white trunks, Harlem's own favorite son, the Golden Boy of fistiana, Joe Wellington!

(JOE enters his corner, dully, with his handlers.)

And may the better man emerge triumphant!

REFEREE: All right, boys, come in the center. You both know the rules, I want the punches kept high and

in the event of a knockdown I want you to go to a
neutral corner. Let's go, and have a good clean fight.

(*The fight itself is a dance, to drums and music and
crowd roar.*

In the first round JOE, *listless, is clobbered, while
the crowd screams; when he is knocked down a
voice cuts through with,* "Kill the bum!" JOE *is
knocked down a second time, this voice is joined by
others,* "Kill the bum! Kill him!" *and only the bell
saves* JOE; *his handlers drag him to his stool and
work on him.*

Between rounds LOPEZ *refuses to sit, but dances to
and around* JOE *in a fever of brute eagerness.*

In the second round JOE *is staggered again, and a
rhythmic chant begins,* "Kill him! Kill him!"
Floored once more, JOE *crawls to haul himself up
by the ropes; what he hears now piercing through
the crowd's roar are the voices of the past—*WELL-
INGTON, *"I give you every word to fight," and* TOM,
"You crazy black bastard," and LORNA, *"I love* TOM,
*tell him what?"—and the crowd's chant is reduced
to its essential,* "Kill! Kill! Kill! Kill!" *It is this, the
basic prehuman need to kill or be killed, that gets
him to his feet. He evades* LOPEZ's *rush, and nails
him with a right which rocks* LOPEZ; *now the tide
turns,* JOE *hitting* LOPEZ *with lefts and rights, while
the same chant of the crowd continues, it is non-
partisan.* LOPEZ *is floored twice; the second time
he is counted out.*

He lies cold, while around him the ring is torn apart, JOE *leaping in victory, handlers and crowd swarming over all in a frenzy of maniacal excitement.)*

9.

The dressing-room returns, in the midst of the yelling and pandemonium; JOE, *with bloody beaten face, is so manicky he is outscreaming all.*

JOE: How about that, how about that? Hallelujah! How about that—

ROXY: My boy, my darling boy, my dear darling boy—

TOKIO: You won a crack at the title, fair and clean, now lay down—

JOE: I'm gonna go outside my weight and beat up the whole damn world!

EDDIE: The world is your oyster now, baby!

JOE: Get Tom in here, I'll grind his bones to make my bread!

ROXY: Darling, how you gave it to him! Not to my enemies!

TOKIO: Lemme fix that eye, Joe—

(*An* OFFICIAL *enters.*)

JOE: I'm gonna beat up the whole damn world! Hallelujah!

OFFICIAL: Joe, the commissioner wants to see you upstairs.

JOE: Let him come down here, anybody wants to see me, here I am!

OFFICIAL: Lopez is out.

JOE: You bet he's out, I put him out! Hallelujah!

OFFICIAL: I mean he's dead.

(*There is instant silence. The* OFFICIAL *exits.*)

JOE [STUPEFIED]: Dead?

TOKIO [LONG PAUSE]: You didn't foul him, you're a clean fighter, anything happened it's an accident—

EDDIE [PAUSE]: There's nothing to worry about.

ROXY [PAUSE]: That's right—

(JOE *in a daze crosses the room, sits apart on a bench, his back to them.*)

EDDIE [TO A HENCHMAN]: Go out there and see what's going on—

(*A* REPORTER *and a* PHOTOGRAPHER *run in.*)

REPORTER: Congratulations, great fight—

(*The* PHOTOGRAPHER *snaps a flashlight shot, and* EDDIE *knocks the camera out of his hands.*)

EDDIE: Get out!

(*They run out.*)

TOKIO: Don't blame yourself for nothing, Joe—

JOE [DAZED]: That poor guy—that poor guy—
ROXY: It's in the hands of God, a thing like that—
JOE: —that poor guy—

(*Other* REPORTERS *and* PHOTOGRAPHERS *pour in; more flashbulbs go off.*)

REPORTER: Hey, Joe, how about a statement—
EDDIE: Outside! Everybody out, the kid's in a state of shock, let him calm himself—
TOKIO: Don't blame yourself, Joe—

(EDDIE *is herding them all out, but* LORNA *comes in past him; he grabs her elbow.*)

EDDIE: You too, Mrs. Moody. In particular.

(LORNA *throws his hand off, and runs to* JOE. EDDIE *looks at them sharply, and exits.* LORNA *kneels to* JOE *in a fierce embrace of his knees.*)

LORNA: Joe—
JOE: —that poor guy—
LORNA [SHAKING HIM]: It wasn't your fault, Joe, you didn't mean it—

(*But* JOE *is lost, uncontactable, muttering from another world:*)

JOE: Whose fault—whose fault—

(*And when he stares at his hands he sees them as if for the first time, alien objects, bloody, and he rises away from* LORNA, *who falls on her knees; he turns this way, that.)*

I gotta—get out, I gotta—run, move—

(He finds himself at a locker bench, and gathers an armful of clothes.)

—get in my car, speed—I gotta get out of my—skin—

LORNA: Joe!

(JOE sees her now, at last, and cries to her in despair:)

JOE: Oh Lorna, why couldn't you love me right?

(And he turns blindly, staggering against the bench, and runs reeling off. LORNA *falls on her face on her fists.*

Blackout.)

10.

In the blackness there is the roar of a car, then a long-drawn-out screech of brakes climaxing in a massive crash, a prolonged human scream, and an auto horn blaring on and on as if no hand lives to stop it; when a siren follows this, what comes out of the darkness is at first only the red rooflight of a police car, turning, turning.

This fades, as the lights come up on the Harlem street again. It is night, and FRANK and LORNA are standing outside a stoop; FRANK takes off his jacket, and covers LORNA's shoulders. They wait. From the stoop WELLINGTON emerges, struggling to get a jacket on over his pajama-top; FRANK moves to help him, and WELLINGTON sits in a stupefaction of collapse on the step.

WELLINGTON: Killed—
FRANK: He was alone in the car, Pa. He died—right away—
WELLINGTON: My Joe—killed.

(He shakes his head, unbelieving.)

What waste—

LORNA: Yes. What waste.

(FRANK *helps his father to his feet.*)

FRANK: Come, Pa. We'll—bring Joe home—
WELLINGTON [WHEN HE CAN]: Yeah—where he belongs—
LORNA: Oh my God, he belonged anywhere—anywhere
a human being could—walk—

(*And because she herself cannot quite walk,* WELL-
INGTON *puts out his hand for her; she takes it, and
they cross out,* LORNA *between the two men.*

Curtain, end of the play.)

AFTERWORD: CREDITS

INVARIABLY the text of a Broadway play is more collaboratively arrived at than the authorship indicates; in a musical the collaboration is manifold. It was particularly so in ours, which was something of an instant musical. I solicited and made use of the advice of everyone, from the least member of the cast up, and the foregoing text bears the thumbprints of too many hands to specify.

In general, the dialogue in the scenes proper is either Odets' or mine; some bits are by Lee Adams, who of course wrote all the lyrics, and most of the dialogue inside the songs by him and Charles Strouse is theirs. Much of the restructuring of the show's musical profile was the contribution of Herb Ross, working with Hillard Elkins and Arthur Penn. A goodly number of lines I took out of the mouths of Penn and Elkins, without much struggle; in the rewriting of the rewriting both were indispensable on the overall, and indeed the structural counselling of playwrights is a forte of Penn's. The final rewrite was much influenced by the friendly criticism of Elliot Norton, who at our invitation came from Boston to New York to confer with us on what we had accomplished in the interim, and informed us it was not enough. Some of the most telling lines were ad-libbed by Sammy Davis, who also suggested the content of many crucial moments, and hauled me out of more than one pitfall; he said to me one night, "I leave you with two words," and paused for me to guess what they were, but I was wrong as well as indelicate, for he then divulged them, "Write colored," and I was much encouraged by his conviction that if I only tried hard enough I could become one of the country's leading colored writers.

W. G.